The Country Club

❖

Why Switching from the Big City to the Boondocks Could Be Your Smartest Move Ever

Dale Wildman

Silvercat Publications
San Diego, California

copyright © 1992 by Dale Wildman

All rights reserved. This work may not be copied, stored, reproduced, retrieved, or transmitted by any means without prior, written permission of the author, except for brief passages quoted in review. For information contact Silvercat Publications, 4070 Goldfinch St., Suite C, San Diego, CA 92103.

GREEN ACRES THEME **Words and Music by Vic Mizzy**

Copyright (c) 1965 Orion Music Publishing, Inc.
Administered by Next Decade Entertainment, Inc.
All Rights Reserved. Used by Permission.

Cover art and design by Tom Voss Illustration, San Diego, CA

First Printing, August 1992   10 9 8 7 6 5 4 3 2 1

Library of Congress Cataloging-in-Publication Data

Wildman, Dale, 1954-
   The country club : why switching from the big city to the boondocks could be your smartest move ever / Dale Wildman
      p.   cm.
            ISBN 0-9624945-5-0 : $8.95
   1. Sociology, Rural—United States. 2. Country life—United States. 3. United States—Rural conditions. I. Title.
HT421.W37 1992
307.72'0973—dc20   92-61455
                                                                CIP

Printed in the United States of America

DEDICATION

❖

To my father, Delmer Wildman (1917-1987), my mother, Laura, and assorted Wildman family members everywhere.

TABLE OF CONTENTS

Preface . . . . *vii*

Introduction 3

CHAPTER I: Over The Rainbow
(Some whys and wheres about moving to the country) 7

CHAPTER II: Hey, Look It Over
(Finding the right place in the right part of the country) 23

CHAPTER III: Drive Time
(Transportation and other ways of gettin' from here to there) 43

CHAPTER IV: MoneyMoneyMoneyMoney
(Making bucks in the boondocks) 59

CHAPTER V: "I'm Telling You, Maurice, The Fatback Is Sublime..."
(The joys of eating in the country) 79

CHAPTER VI: That's Entertainment
(Things to do in the country) 95

CHAPTER VII: Won't You Be My Neighbor?
(People, life, and living in the country.) 109

CHAPTER VIII: Very Real, Very Rural
(A personal look at some of the immeasureable aspects of country living.) 121

APPENDIX *129*

Preface

When I mention the "Big City" in the following pages, I am referring not only to America's giant and not-so-giant metropolises, but also to the numerous and crowded suburbs that are becoming more numerous and more crowded every day. Our cities and the suburbs that surround them share many of the same problems to varying degrees. And they are peopled, for the most part, by folks who are more or less in the same socioeconomic boat.

Likewise, when I talk about the "Boondocks," I am not just speaking about lonely mountaintops in Tennessee, abandoned outposts in the middle of Montana, or dugouts in the Alaskan wilderness. Boondocks refers more generally to the rural but not completely isolated areas of our nation, those small towns and villages which are located far from the "maddening" crowd—but not so far that you can't find a good Pizza Hut when you need one.

And, the "Country Club"?

That refers to all those people who have already made the smartest move they might ever make for themselves, the move to the Boondocks.

Introduction

Green Acres is the place to be,
Fa-arm livin', that's the life for me,
Land spreadin' out so far and wide,
Keep Manhattan, just give me that countryside . . .
—Lyrics from TV's *Green Acres*

No doubt about it. That Eddie Albert was one smart cookie.

I don't mean to imply that it's all "City, bad...Country, good!" Not at all. I lived in cities for years. I like cities. They offer lots of important advantages and are filled with good and decent and hardworking people.

Besides, where else can you get oyster soup at three o'clock in the morning?

But...

The many problems dominating life in today's overcrowded metropolitan areas are as familiar as the headlines: crime...drugs...violence...child kidnappings and molestations...rape...AIDS...gangs...the plight of the homeless...air pollution...water pollution...traffic jams. The list goes on.

There's also the cost. Living in the average Big City is expensive. Real estate prices are ludicrous, rental rates beyond ludicrous, the simple cost of daily living outrageous. Many people are only a job loss away from personal or family disaster. For those who have already lost jobs they had built lifestyles around and now find themselves "on the street," the situation is nothing short of desperate.

For many, the city has become irrelevant to the truly important things in life. While growing numbers of people are aching to belong and to participate, the city offers them only more impersonal agencies and institutions. And that's all it can do, because the city is just too damn big for human-scale solutions. In urbs and suburbs across the country, people have become official nobodies—clients, constituents, numbers—and they don't like it. Some find escape in the gang; some in the women's auxiliary or the rotisserie baseball league; some in the bars on the windows and the shotgun under the bed. Many others are saying: "Enough! We're outta here!"

It's true that some of these problems can be encountered anywhere by anybody. But face it: they're much more likely to be found in our urban areas. By statistics alone, the Big City has become a dangerous, expensive place to live for ourselves and our children. And ou can't even begin to measure the cost in peace of mind.

There comes a time when oyster soup just isn't that important.

So is this a call for a mass exodus, exhorting city-dwellers and suburbanites to flee in search of safety and sanity elsewhere?

No. For one thing, many Big City people are quite happy and satisfied with their lives. Some, who may be dissatisfied, may also resist the notion of change or feel that they're too old or too established to try something new. Others simply don't want to live anywhere but the cities. Somehow, I just can't see Ralph Cramden embracing life in Flora, Illinois. Then, too, some people need to live in cities to work at their chosen professions, like window washers or U.N. ambassadors.

However, there are many reasons to believe that lots of people would be much happier living their lives in what I call the Boondocks, those vast rural areas of our nation. Already, growing numbers of people have joined the "back to basics" revolution in America, moving to less populated, less noisy, less dangerous, less expensive locales and discovering a higher quality of life as a result.

But, if it's so worthwhile, why haven't more people made the move? In part it may be because there are so many overwhelming misconceptions about life in the Boondocks. Some people act as if there would be "nothing to do" if they lived "out there"—no jobs, no opportunities, no amusements, no entertainment, no social life, no sophistication, no culture, no civilization, no nothing.

This is not true. Not by a long shot. I'm convinced that if more people knew what life really was like "out there," many more would give it a try. And, in the process, improve their social and economic circumstances and create happier, healthier, more productive lives for themselves and their families.

So convinced, in fact, that I've written a book about it.

In the following pages, I'll discuss what I feel to be the most important of the many reasons for living in the country. I'll also get a little into the "hows" of living in the country as well. The "whys" help to serve as motivation for people to explore the benefits of rural life while the "hows" offer some of the specifics for going about it.

I wrote this book, in part, to share my own love for the country as well as to correct some of the misconceptions about rural life. But, more than this, I wrote it to help people decide if moving to the boondocks would be good for them. After all, moving to the country is a big step, especially for people who have only their imaginations and their urban discouragements to guide them. It's wise to proceed slowly and intelligently so that the head and the heart can work together.

I'm the first to say that country living is not for everybody. But if you find yourself facing some of the overwhelming problems of an overpopulated society; if you are fed up with and worn down by excessive worrying about everything from your job to your children's education to the smog index; if there are times when you feel that you would just like to get out from under and start all over again in a place where you can grow and prosper and find a parking space...

Well, you just might start by reading the rest of this book.

CHAPTER I

Over The Rainbow

❖

(Some whys and wheres about moving to the country)

Those Troublemakers, Adam and Eve

Lord, we got trouble.
 You leave a man and a woman alone in a garden, and look what happens.
 People happen. And happen. And keep on happening.
 And look what's become of the garden. We've got people to the left of us. People to the right of us. People behind us, in front of us, over us, and below us. Listening through our walls and walking across our lawns, crowding our streets and clogging our highways, taking our parking places and grabbing our taxis.
 How many people, you ask? Try 253.6 million, according to U.S. Census Bureau estimates, all living on 3,539,289 square miles of land area, which averages out to nearly 72 people per square mile. Of course, this average is a lot higher in urban areas—New York City has 64,992 people per square mile—and that's just at

last count. There are more people by now, and it's a pretty safe bet there are still more on the way.

If only Eve had known about Norplant.

She didn't, though, and what she and Adam started isn't going to stop. In fact, barring some sort of miracle or catastrophe of Biblical proportions, it is no doubt going to get worse. As time goes on, there will be more and more people, all crowding in on less and less available land area. They'll be squeezing into condos and stacking up in apartment buildings and coming to formation in tract housing all across America (not to mention sprawling on heating grates and sleeping in subway stations). Our overpopulated, overcrowded cities and suburbs are only going to get more overpopulated and overcrowded. And the problems we have come to take for granted from overpopulation and overcrowding are only going to get worse.

"Horse feathers," you say? Or horse-something. Well, since the late 1960s, American population has increased at the rate of about 1 per cent per annum. Some years a little more, some years a little less, but always right around there, and never less than 0.9 per cent a year. Despite the growing use and acceptance of safe, practical birth control methods and the economic necessity of smaller families, the fact is we're still pumping out people in record numbers. And as far as land area goes, except maybe for Antarctica, there aren't any more Alaskas to be purchased on this planet. What we have now is it.

"So what?" you reply. Wise men in ivory towers tell us that our birth rate is shrinking. The key word there is *rate*. The term *shrinking birth rate* makes it sound as if there are fewer people being born. But all it really means is that we're not cranking them out quite so fast as we used to. Think about this: In 1965 there were some 3.801 million people born in our country; in 1990, the figure was 3.731 million. Some shrinkage.

True, the United Nations says that we can expect the U.S. population to level off at about 320 million by the year 2110. That's hard to imagine, since population has never leveled off before, but that's what they say. Still, this comes from the same people who didn't know the Berlin Wall was going down until somebody started knocking big holes in it with a sledgehammer. And even if by some miracle they turn out to be right, what good does that do those of us who will be checking out long before then? Or our children? Or their children, for that matter? Overcrowding is a big problem getting bigger, with no apparent relief in sight.

Consider China, where overpopulation has reached critical mass. Many provinces require that couples who have a second child forfeit fifteen per cent of their salaries until the child is seven years old. It gets even worse if they have a third child. Nobody seems to know just what happens after that, but suffice it to say it's no place for the Waltons.

So What's The Answer?

The good news is that its not all bad news. The urban fast lane is not the only alternative. There is still plenty of garden available in the U.S. and plenty of advantages to be had for those who choose to move there.

Consider that about 75 per cent of our 253.6 million people live in or around our most densely populated areas—the cities and their metropolitan areas. That leaves plenty of acreage in plenty of small towns and villages for those who want to pursue what many think is a better life for themselves and their families.

Is Country Life Really "Better"?

That "better quality of life" argument always brings a knee-jerk howl from defenders of city life, so let's head that off right here. Nobody's saying that moving to the country is some sort of panacea or magic bullet for all of life's problems. If your kids had acne when you lived in L.A., they're *still* going to have acne if you move to the country. (Unless their acne was caused by smog.)

But what this means is that a much more satisfying way of life *may* await those who are willing to relocate to the country. Now, those who disbelieve that a "better life" can be found in the country are always quick to ask for some sort of proof—preferably something hard, fast, and quantitative—to support such claims. It's true that this is the sort of thing that's hard to quantify. It's also true that some statisticians, given enough time and numbers, can prove to you that Rhode Island is bigger than Texas. But to satisfy the nay-sayers, let's take a statistical look at a few subjects that have become of increasing concern to many Americans.

Take violent crime. When President Bush, in his 1992 State of the Union speech, singled out street crime as one of the nation's major problems, we all knew he meant city streets, not country roads. (Though it must be admitted that some of the other things he said are open to debate.) Statistics? The U.S. Justice Department defines violent crime as murder, rape, aggravated assault, robbery, burglary, and various other acts of illegal violence. In 1990, there were no fewer than 1,430,085 violent crimes *reported* in American cities. The suburbs *reported* an additional 205,987 incidents of violence. The figure for rural areas? 55,815.

Doubting Thomases and Thomasinas will race to point out that, since there are more people in the cities and suburbs, the violent crime totals for such metropolitan areas would naturally be higher when compared to places with homes where the buffalo would roam, if there were any roaming buffalo left. Fair enough, but flawed.

The trouble with that little objection is that, when you break those figures down by population, the "better life" advantages of this particular aspect of country living stand out like a haywagon on Wall Street. Those 1990 statistics for violent crimes tell us that 965 murders, rapes, etc. were committed against every 100,000 city residents. Suburbanites were victimized at the rate of 449 per 100,000. Country folk: 209 per 100,000.

Life is not all violent crime, you say? Right, we also have drugs. True, a lot of street crime is drug-related, and it's hard to separate the two. But you really don't have to, because where is the drug problem most pervasive? According to the NIDA (National Institute on Drug Abuse) and national drug czar, Bob Martinez, cocaine use is rising fastest in—where else?—the cities. Among certain urban groups, such drug use has leapt eighteen per cent over last year, while dramatic increases were registered in cocaine- and heroin-related visits to hospital emergency rooms. Moreover, new figures show that the effort to curb hard-core abuse has slowed and will likely become more and more ineffective as increasing numbers of longtime, casual users lapse into addiction.

As distressing as all this is, it's hard to believe that any of it would astonish anybody. That doesn't mean that every urban or suburban dweller is experimenting with better living through chemicals, and it's not as if there aren't more than a few country boys slipping behind the barn for a fast doobie or two. But obviously, drug use is a lot more common in metropolitan areas, just like street crime and a lot of other societal ills. You don't find crack houses in Bugtussle.

More "Good" News: Most People Won't Listen

Citing a mountain of statistics on urban problems really isn't necessary, anyway. Most Americans already have a sense that life in the country is something special.

According to a 1986 Gallup poll, over half of all metropolitan residents would rather live in the country. A recent survey of baby-boomers, by a shoe company of all things (PF Flyers), found that a majority want less hectic lifestyles, and "wish they had more time with their children." The less-hurried pace and less-harried lifestyle of country living may well be what they're looking for.

There's more. *Time* magazine reports that research has shown some 61 per cent of Americans say that "earning a living today requires so much effort that it's difficult to find time to enjoy life," while 89 per cent said it was more important these days to spend time with their families. Again, country life could be the answer.

So if, as *Time* claims, "Americans are rediscovering the joys of home life, basic values and things that last," does this mean that droves of people are moving back to the countryside, where such a lifestyle is almost certainly more easily found than in America's bustling and demanding cities and suburbs?

Heck, no. Not by a darn sight.

Recent findings indicate that, while the inner-city is losing population, the road out of the metropolis dead-ends in the suburbs. People continue to remain in urban areas. Combined with immigration and those rural few chasing some Big City pipe dream, our urban population is actually increasing—it went up about 1.5 per cent between 1980 and 1990. Despite the very real "back-to-basics" movement sweeping the nation; despite all those people who claim to want to move to the country; despite the flood of verifiable, easily recognizable, and just plain common-sense-and-common-knowledge information about what country living has to offer, almost nobody is listening. Instead, they're looking to the already overcrowded suburbs for salvation. Out of the skillet into the sauce pan. Suburbs might look good compared to cities, but its only relative. The "burbs" already suffer from many of the same dangers and frustrations as urban areas, as well as problems of their own.

So why is this good news? Because that leaves more of the countryside ready and waiting for those willing enough or gutsy enough to take advantage of it. Many of those abandoning the city for the suburbs are on to something. They just aren't taking it far enough to get the results they are looking for. And most of them never will—the urban population of the United States hasn't decreased since the early 1800s. As selfish and cynical as it sounds, this is good news because it guarantees that there will always be country land for some people to dream about and a few others to take advantage of.

Does Anybody Really Know What Time It Is?

So is *anyone* waking up and smelling the cider when it comes to the distinct advantages of rural living? Oh my, yes. Despite the noted influx of people into the suburbs, there are many who have already felt the call of the great countryside and acted on it. Nearly eighty per cent of U.S. population was centered around metropolitan areas in the early 1980s compared to only seventy-five per cent today.

It would be simple to cite case history after case history. To tell you of Barry Blake, the liquor industry big-shot (no pun intended) who left his job and moved from his luxurious Manhattan penthouse to experience the joys of running an apple mill in picturesque Vermont. Or of Jason and Mary Kovatch, who loved living and working in Pasadena, California so much that they moved 94 miles away, to the small mountain town of Frazier Park, and who now say of their time spent living in the city, "it was a zoo."

Such examples would be useful to illustrate that it is more than possible to trade the frustrations of metropolitan living for life in the country and come out ahead. They would let others know—let you know—about some of the people who have done it, why they did it, and how they are enjoying it.

All of which would be important for one very good reason: it would help you decide whether or not you would like to do it yourself. It is tempting to argue that almost everyone would be happier and better off away from the problems of modern urban/suburban living. But let's be realistic: there are many who would not—could not, perhaps—make the adjustment. And, like any move, going from "Big City" to "Boondocks" does take adjustment. So, despite the success enjoyed by the many other people who have picked up, packed up, and moved to quieter, more rustic climes, the first thing you should ask yourself is, "Would this be the right move for me and mine?"

If you suspect, even a little, that the answer might be "yes," please, please read on.

Which Way Do I Go, Which Way Do I Go?

Good question. There's an awful lot of country in this land of ours, and anyone deciding they might want to enjoy the benefits of rural living has a whole continent to choose from, and then some. Of course, you don't just

> **Making A Smooth Move**
>
> Whoever said three moves is as good as a fire gave fire way too much credit. Between damage, outright breakage, and complete loss, *one* average move can cause more destruction than fans of Mrs. O'Leary's cow could ever dream of.
>
> Fortunately, there are some things you can do to take the pain out of Moving Day. Here are a few tips for a successful move:
>
> - If you're packing your things yourself, and especially if you and a crew of friends are doing the moving, a larger number of lighter bundles is better than a smaller number of heavier ones. Your friends will thank you. So will your back.
> - Get boxes from grocery stores. Beg, borrow, steal, or buy furniture pads and covers from a truck-rental dealer.
> - Mark fragile items FRAGILE in big, bold letters. Professional movers usually won't accept liability for broken items that homeowners packed themselves.
> - Make an inventory list, especially if you're having the job done by professional movers. Discuss the inventory with the movers beforehand, pointing out the more valuable items.

pick up and move. The advantages and characteristics of one rural area can be mightily different from those of another, so the idea is to match up your own personal style and preferences with the place you move to.

In deciding what part of the country you might want to settle in, it may help to answer some questions about population density—such as, "what are the most populous areas right now?" and "what areas are people moving to?"—and to consider factors like the available land area, the urban/rural breakdown of the present population, and any other facts, figures, conventional wisdom, or prevailing impressions you can track down about the region you're considering. The following general overview of the U.S. will provide you with some of the information you need. You can seek out more specifics once you decide if and where you're going.

Despite a definite shift westward, the Northeast section of the United States still has the greatest concentration of population. The West, though, is by far the nation's fastest-growing region, with a 1980s population jump of 22 per cent—more than twice the national rate—compared to 13.5 per cent growth in the South, 3.4 per cent in the Northeast and 1.3 per cent in the Midwest. The West also has the nation's highest birth rate, as well as the highest percentage of residents under age 18.

By state, Nevada boasted the West's greatest population increase during the last decade—there are 50 per cent more Nevadans now—followed by Alaska, Arizona, California, New Mexico, Utah, Washington, Hawaii, Colorado, Oregon, Idaho and Montana. As you might expect, Alaska still has the nation's largest rural land area (569,733.3 sq. miles), and for obvious reasons, it will probably remain very sparsely populated for a long time.

Breaking down urban and rural populations by region, the Northeast is 75.2 per cent urban and 24.8 per cent rural—a lot like the nation as a whole. The Midwest splits 71.7 per cent urban and 28.3 per cent rural. The South leads the nation in rural population, with 31.4 per cent as compared to its 68.6 per cent urban residents. (By state, though, Vermont, with 67.8 per cent, has the highest percentage of rural population.) And the West, largely because of heavily populated California and Hawaii, has the densest urban population, (86.3 per cent).

Averages can be misleading. No matter what the figures, every state has its share of rural space. A word or two, however, about California and Hawaii: *be careful*. Although there are still rural areas in both states, both are filling up fast. Large parts of California are virtually uninhabitable because they are inhospitable, inaccessible, or used for ordnance testing. In addition, Hawaii is a pretty far stretch, both financially and geographically, for most people. If your heart is truly set on hula girls and overpriced souvenirs, the Hawaii Settler's Bureau offers an informative guide to moving there.

As regards population, Southern California in particular has about reached the saturation point. Seems like everybody wants to live with Johnny Carson, and he just hasn't got the room. It comes as no surprise, then, that California has the largest urban land area (8,175,4 sq. miles) and the highest proportion of urban population (92.6 per cent) in the U.S.

Not even rural Northern California is immune to the strangling effects of Southern California's megapolitan tentacles. In fact, the northern part of the state has been described as a rural revolution in the making. Because urban voters dominate state politics, folks in California's rural north feel they've been getting the short end of the stick in everything from garbage collection to library closings. It's gotten to the point that some politicians have authored a "State of Northern California" proposal calling for California to be split in two, creating a fifty-first state in the north!

There aren't likely to be fifty-one stars on "Old Glory" anytime soon, but it's one example of why you can't assume that "rural is rural." Find out everything you can about any area of the nation that you might consider, carefully evaluating the pros and cons, and go from there.

One other thing: finding a rural area in which to hang your hammock doesn't mean you have to move a million miles from where you are now. As noted, virtually every state offers rural room to roam around, settle down, and set up housekeeping in. You don't have to deplete your bank account and your body moving far from friends and relatives just to get away from it all. Oz might be a great place to live, but even Dorothy came to realize that real happiness was available right in her own back yard (which just happened to be located in rural Kansas). Besides, moving out of state involves additional red tape. For example, vehicle plates must be transferred; in some cases, insurance companies need to be changed; first-year income tax must often be figured on a partial basis, both for the state you're leaving and the one you're moving to. None of these are major hassles. But if a great piece of rural land lies comparatively near-by, why set up more hoops to jump through than necessary?

In fact, one of the most important reasons to consider staying close to where you live now is those aforementioned friends and relatives. There's nothing wrong with moving six states away, or even all the way across the country, if that's what you want. But moving to a rural area in the same region you live in now makes it easier to keep in contact with the people you want to stay close to. As for those you won't miss, moving just a few hours away is usually sufficient to keep them at bay. At least, you won't be running into them at the market.

Reaching a Climate

Moving to the country won't guarantee you a perfect climate. Geography has a lot more influence over that. In regard to climate, differences between the city and the country are relatively insignificant. Most Illinois farmers dread winter just as much as Chicago aldermen. But even if rural areas can't claim any climatic advantages, the prevailing climate is going to have an

> **Establishing Residency**
>
> If you're moving to another state, it's a good idea to establish legal residency as soon as you can. If you or a member of your family is attending a state college or university, this will help you qualify for in-state college tuition fees or waivers or other state-sponsored programs. And it's always good for tax purposes so you don't get stuck with taxes in a state where you no longer reside.
>
> Several steps will help you establish residency in your new home state:
> - Ask the local county clerk for a "Certificate of Domocile."
> - Get a driver's license and register your car in your new state.
> - Register to vote immediately and cast a ballot in your new state at the first opportunity.
> - File state and federal income taxes in your new state.

impact on your lifestyle and your sense of being part of the great outdoors, wherever you choose to live.

Generally speaking, you probably already know a lot more about geography and climate than you may think. For instance, nobody has to tell you it gets hot in Florida and cold in Montana. Or that it snows in the Rocky Mountains and rains in Seattle. Or that you're more likely to see a hurricane on the East Coast than in Kansas, where tornadoes may make you pine for a nice, quiet hurricane or a gentle, rolling earthquake.

For the most part, the West Coast is known for its mildness along the coast. But if you head east beyond a mountain range or two or even further into Nevada, Colorado, or New Mexico, things get pretty hot and dry. That's why every third uncle with serious asthma or hay fever daydreams about Arizona. (Note to asthmatics and hay-fever sufferers: the Desert Southwest isn't the Godsend it used to be for you. The pollen index is still good, if not as good as before, and you're still better off living here than rolling around in a Missouri hayfield. But, so many people have moved into the area, planting trees and seeding lawns, that there are far more problem-causing allergens than ever before. Which reaffirms the wisdom of looking before you leap.)

If you settle in the Rocky Mountains, take a blanket—there's cold in them thar hills in the winter and lots of snow to go with it. That makes it good for winter sports, though, and the summers are crisp, sunny, and really quite pleasant.

The region of the country weathermen call the Great Interior—Montana, the Dakotas, and parts of Minnesota, Wisconsin, Nebraska and Iowa—can experience hot, hot summers and long, bitterly-cold winters. As you head south through Kansas and Missouri, things get a little milder, and you tend to get less precipitation—that's a fifty-cent word for rain and snow—but it still gets cold in the winter and mighty hot in the summer. If you really like it hot, though, try Oklahoma, Arkansas and the rest of the South. And if you don't mind humidity and mosquitoes, check out the Southern gulf and border states.

Eastward from Kansas and Missouri through the rest of the traditional Midwest, the change of the four seasons becomes more pronounced, and the overall climate becomes a good deal milder. Nevertheless, it can get hot enough for you to start wondering about the costs of laying in central-air and sometimes cold enough to make you bring your brass monkey inside, especially in Wisconsin, Michigan, and the northern parts of Illinois, Indiana, and Ohio.

After all this, it still has to be admitted that there are no hard-and-fast rules. For example, few places get colder than parts of Northern New England, particularly Maine. Or hotter than certain places in New York state. And, Alaska, which can be quintessentially cold

> ### Hay Fever
>
> It doesn't cause a fever. It doesn't even come from hay. But, for those susceptible to it, hay fever can be a major country aggravation.
> Hay fever is an allergic reaction to certain minute, airborne particles from seed-bearing trees, grasses, and weeds. It causes sore throats, red eyes, runny noses, and lots of sneezing. Except for Alaska and the southern half of Florida, no area of the United States is completely free of hay fever. The temperate regions, where grasses and trees without flowers predominate, are about the worst. Because farming disrupts the soil and encourages the growth of troublemakers like ragweed, America's heartland, from the Rockies to the Appalachians and from Canada down to the Mid-South, is a hay fever hot spot.

north of the Arctic Circle, offers a comparatively mild climate along its southern coast.

Tornadoes and Hurricanes and Earthquakes, Oh My

It's not likely, but it could happen; so if getting caught in a natural disaster is one of your major worries, consider the following:

When it comes to tornadoes, the states that have reported the most are Kansas (Remember Dorothy?), Oklahoma, and Texas. But almost every state has had a tornado or three in recent memory. Hurricanes originate at sea, usually in late summer or fall, and primarily strike the Gulf states and southern Atlantic coast before moving north, generally following the coast as far as New England. California and the Pacific Northwest are most prone to earthquakes, along with parts of Montana, Idaho, and Missouri of all places.

The point is this: No matter where you live, someone is going to tell you about the quake of '72, the tidal wave of '56, the floods of '48, '63, and '87, the killer storm of 1708, or something else that makes the area a real trouble spot. No one wants to make light of natural disasters—after all, they're not called disasters for nothing. But statistically speaking, you're probably in about the same amount of danger wherever you bed down.

There is a difference, however. High-rise apartment tenants are pretty much trapped whenever an earthquake, hurricane, or tornado comes roaring through. TV broadcasters have to crawl under their desks for shelter. Urbanites have to watch out for falling debris and glass.

Country folk just go down to the basement and wait it out.

CHAPTER II

Hey, Look It Over

❖

(Finding the right place in the right part of the country)

Sticking it To the Tax Man

If one of the reasons you're contemplating a move to the country is to escape a brutal urban tax burden, you're not alone.

A recent *Money* magazine poll reported that six per cent of respondents had moved simply to escape what they considered exorbitant taxes—and another twenty-two per cent were considering it! One of the greatest middle-class joys is giving the tax man the middle finger, and a lot of Americans are in the mood to do just that.

Surprisingly, the problem isn't so much Uncle Sam as state and local bureaucrats. Some of the frustration stems from state taxes, which are rising faster than federal taxes almost everywhere. But with increasing frequency, larger and larger tax bites are being taken by municipal governments. In fact, local taxes are higher than ever and prevailing expectations are that they're going even higher. One editor of a state newsletter on taxes and budgets agrees with most tax experts that "...local taxes pose a far greater threat" and that both state and local taxes are "much more likely to rise each year" than federal. All this while state and local services are being cut to the rib cage—the trend is more and higher taxes for less and fewer of the services, such as police and fire protection, that taxes are supposed to pay for.

A move to the country, at least within your current state, isn't likely to alter your state tax burden. But finding a state with a lower tax rate than where you're living now probably means a switch to a state classified as rural (if you don't already live in one). According to *Money* magazine, New York has the highest property tax in the nation. The three states with the lowest property tax rates are Alaska—where those over age 65 don't pay any at all—Nevada, and Wyoming, in that order. (These three states are also included with Idaho, Montana, Nebraska, the Dakotas, Kansas, Missouri, Utah, Colorado, and Vermont as the states with the largest number of rural counties.)

In addition, five states currently levy no state-wide sales or use taxes: Alaska, Delaware, Montana, New Hampshire, and Oregon. And nine states still have no income tax: New Hampshire, South Dakota, Tennessee, Texas, Washington, Alaska, Florida, Nevada, and Wyoming. (New Hampshire may have enacted one by the time you read this, however, and it already ranks tenth-highest nationally in property taxes, so be advised.)

One couple, profiled in a national magazine, became so fed up with the state and local taxes they had to pay in San Diego, California that they packed up the kid, sold the house, and moved to the foothills of the Rocky Mountains in the wilds of Wyoming. Result: $3,000 less per year in combined state and property taxes. And there are many more people making the same sort of move for the same sort of reasons.

The clincher here is local taxes. In the country, many small towns and villages levy—are you ready?—*no municipal taxes whatsoever*. Which means that if you live in the right state and the right rural location, you pay no state or local taxes at all. None at all. (One small reminder: Don't let appearances fool you. Boise, Idaho, may sound as rural as all get-out—until you arrive and find yourself hemmed in among 125,000 other Boiseians, and paying the taxes to prove it. Make sure your rural haven really is rural before you start planning your move there.)

As Arthur Godfrey said, "I'm proud to be paying taxes in the United States—the only thing is, I could be just as proud for half the money."

Land, Lots o' Land

It's not just taxes that living in the country will lower. In general, the farther you get from the city, the less you're going to pay for real estate.

To look at it a little more scientifically, remember the discussion of "population density" in the first chapter? Well, that's what to watch for. Or rather, watch *out* for, because the greater the population density, the higher the land prices.

This even holds true in comparing one city to another. Take New York City, for example, singled out above for its crushing population density. Right now, in 1992, land in New York City is running about $3500 per square foot. One square foot of Dallas, Texas, on the other hand, will cost you around $300, which is still way too much but a steal compared to Big Apple real estate.

Meanwhile, farm land, buildings and all, can be had, on average, for some $690 an acre. *An acre.* That's 43,560 square feet. (One acre in Central Park would cost $152 million, plus change.) And *farmable* land is generally the most expensive rural real estate. Other rural property can be picked up for even less.

There's more good news. Many programs, on both the state and federal level, are specifically designed to help with the purchase of rural real estate. Not everybody qualifies, of course, and in some cases the conditions for eligibility can be pretty stringent and specific. But it can be done.

Alaska, for example, has something called a Homestead Program which offers up to 160 acres of state-owned land to would-be homesteaders. You can pay fair market value. Or you can earn complete title simply by "proving up," which generally means surveying, constructing a permanent dwelling of some kind, and establishing residence there for at least twenty-five months out of the first five years.

You might prefer Maine. Frenchboro is a tiny community on a small island off the Maine coast. Last word had it that the state housing authority was offering new homesites, houses and all, on one to one-and-a-half acre lots, on a very reasonable ($330 a month) three-year lease-with-option-to-buy basis, as a way of boosting the island's year-round population. Now, life in a fishing village can be a little on the rugged side. More than a few people have tried it and couldn't hack it. But, if you think you're hardy enough, this could be the deal for you.

Maine and Nevada also provide Rural Housing Programs. These programs work primarily to finance developers of low-income rental housing in rural areas, but if you settle on a place with more than one habitable dwelling, you may be able to work something out. If you are a first-time farmer type, Nebraska offers a First-

Time Farmers Loan to assist in purchases of agricultural real estate.

The federal government also helps out with rural habitation. If you're concerned about the plumbing (or lack of it) in your prospective rural home, and if you meet the age requirement, the Elderly Rural Rehabilitation Program provides grants for installing indoor plumbing facilities. (In case you're interested, the states in which more than 3.2 per cent of homes lack a flush toilet, a bathtub or shower, or hot and cold running water are: New Mexico, Arkansas, Mississippi, Alabama, Georgia, North and South Carolina, Virginia, West Virginia, Kentucky and Tennessee.)

The federal government's largest source of help for rural inhabitants falls under the auspices of the Farmer's Home Administration (FmHA), which is part of the U.S. Department of Agriculture (USDA). At one time in the late seventies, the FmHA had funding available in the amount of some $4 billion dollars. That sort of loot represented a lot of help for a lot of people...until the Reagan Administration, horrified at the amount of money going to God-knows-who, slashed federal support for rural development by 75 per cent. That left about $1 billion, which is where the budget remained under the kinder, gentler Bush administration.

A billion dollars is still a pretty good chunk of change, though, and a number of programs offering loans and grants for rural use have so far escaped the axe. Specifically for farmers, the FmHA offers farm ownership and operating loans, soil and water loans, emergency loans, farm labor housing loans and grants, and state mediation grants, to name just a few.

For rural housing in general, the federal possibilities are impressive. According to the USDA, "FmHA housing credit is available to eligible applicants to buy, build or improve" housing or to provide "affordable rental housing in rural communities..."—that is, communities with populations of less than 10,000, though in some cases FmHA will help out in areas with populations between 10,000 and 20,000. You can apply for low-moderate income housing loans, rural rental housing loans, low-income repairs and grants, rental assistance grants, self-help housing grants, housing preservation grants, housing site development loans, and more. Contact the USDA for specific information on pertinent programs and guidelines.

You Might Want To Try Before You Buy

No matter where in the country you're moving, and no matter how carefully you've analyzed yourself, your desired lifestyle, the place you're moving to, and everything else you want to analyze, there's always a chance that, once you get there, you'll discover that country life is not for you. After all, there are no guarantees in any move, and switching from the city to the country is no exception. Country living, especially if you've been residing in the city for a while, may take some time to get used to. Some people will love it right off and for always. Others will find it, like warm beer or rap music, to be an acquired taste. And some will discover that they really don't care to live in the country at all or that they simply would be happier somewhere else.

If you're not absolutely convinced that the country, with all of its advantages, is your glass of iced tea—and even if you are—you might try renting before you plunk a down payment down and fully commit yourself to a lifestyle you've never tried before. After all, it's better to stick your big toe in the river before you dive in. It makes a fast retreat possible, more convenient, and a whole lot drier to boot.

Besides, renting a place in the country has some advantages all its own. For one thing, the rent itself is shockingly low. For example, inner-city rent for the average one-bedroom apartment in Honolulu is $1300 a month. (Suburban Honolulu offers the same apartment for about $1000 a month.) New York City's average monthly rent for the same apartment is some $775, while Boston's is $665, and Chicago's is $650. Suburban rentals, as in Honolulu, can generally be found for something less than the inner-city rates. Rural rentals are universally less. *A lot* less. Oklahoma, Colorado, Kansas, Texas, Arkansas, and Tennessee offer the most reasonable rental rates. But the fact is, in most rural locales you can find entire houses for less than half the rent you'd expect to pay for a dinky apartment in the typical city.

Moreover, the terms and conditions under which you rent your place in the country—whatever you rent in the country, whether a sleeping room, a cottage, or a three-story house, is always your *place* and never, never your *rental*—are, almost without exception, less stringent than elsewhere. Many times no lease contract is necessary. There are often no first-and-last-month's-rent requirements, pet-or-children restrictions, or any of the other impositions that urban landlords seem to delight in. Rent-in-exchange-for-work arrangements are not unusual. Many country landlords are more than willing to reduce rents even further for tenants who agree to perform specific repairs, maintenance, or general handyman stuff.

Being able to rent without a lease contract is no small thing, because it allows you the freedom to try the country without being legally bound for a set period of time. Not every rural landlord or landlady offers that sort of arrangement, and some will offer it only if they know you. But many country people, resisting formal arrangements of all kinds and preferring to keep things as uncomplicated as possible, would really rather rent out their property without a signed contract. Besides, country folk often pride themselves on being shrewd judges of character, and many still live by the old adage that "a man's (or woman's) word is his bond." So, if you can pass their muster as a decent sort of person, they're often willing to be more than reasonable, both rent-wise and otherwise. True, it might mean a little risk for both parties. But many country folks understand that renting based on trust, not on the mistrust implied by a lease contract, is a simpler and much more pleasant experience for everybody.

Looking For Mr. Good House

Despite the wisdom of hedging your bet by renting before you buy, and despite all the advantages of renting in the country, there will still be those bent on acquiring a place to call their own. Or those who feel that owning ought to be part of their country experience. Or those who come across a purchase deal too sweet to pass up. Like "they" say, "some of the best deals are made in a hurry." So if you stumble into, or shrewdly negotiate, a country-great price for a country-great piece of property, by all means take it. In any case you can always sell. Leaving a country home you have to sell may not be as quick or easy as leaving a rented place—is it anywhere?—but it's hardly impossible.

Okay. You've thought about all this and you've decided to buy in the country anyway. At the very least you've decided to trade in the undeniable problems that come with living in the city for the vastly different if just as real challenges of rural life. You've been watching the nightly news on a regular basis. You know all about the interest rates being way down. And you don't give a darn about renting before you buy.

Fair enough. It might not be such a bad idea after all, and it certainly is a timely one. Interest rates *are* down and inventories are up, and that's the best time to buy if you're going to buy anything. As of this writing, politics and economics make it a buyer's market if you have the resources. Plus, if you already own a house in the city or suburbs, you can peddle it and buy a country place just like it, or even better, and probably have some of your equity left over. Like land, country homes are much less expensive than those in metropolitan areas.

But how to begin the search? One dabbler in rural properties developed what he called the "eleven-farm theory" to safeguard against ill-advised purchases. All he did was to look over ten farms before he bought any. No matter how much he liked any of the first ten, he wouldn't buy. Then he would buy the very next place he looked at that looked better to him than any of those first ten. He claimed never to have bought a loser.

It may not be necessary to go to those extremes, but it does pay to be careful when considering housing anywhere. After all, it's impossible to say what you'll run into until you begin your search. Especially because the country may be rather more unfamiliar to you than most locales, it might not hurt to proceed a little more slowly and carefully than usual.

First off, recognize that help is available if you want it. Real estate agents are everywhere. You can always find one who will look for you, especially if you know just what you want. But, if you have the time, it might be a lot more satisfying, and probably a lot more fun, to look for your own country castle. If nothing else, you won't be quite as disappointed when you drop everything to see some "hot property" that some agent somewhere assured you "won't last at this price." However you choose to search, though, chances are excellent that somewhere in the right region, at the right price, is just-the-right country house waiting to become your home.

Whether you search on your own or use the help of a realtor, knowing just what style of house you're looking for (assuming that you have a preference) can be a big help. You should be aware that moving to the New England region doesn't mean you have to choose a *Cape Cod* and that the style known as *Contemporary Rustic* doesn't exactly conjure up visions of Norman Rockwell.

Happily, there is an enormous variety of house styles and features available in rural America. Traditional styles are more readily found than exotic, but distinctive structures, especially among older homes, are more common than you might think. The aforementioned *Cape Cod*, a one to one-and-a-half story clapboard cottage with no front porch, is quite popular in many parts of the country. So is the *Saltbox*, a two-story clapboard featuring a short-pitched roof in front and a long low slope to the rear, and the large, two-story *Colonial Revival*, with its six-paned windows and open side-porch. You may also encounter some of the classic Victorian styles such as *Carpenter Gothic*, a vertically emphasized two-story, with one, two, or three steeply pitched gables and a bonnet porch, or even a *Queen Anne*, which typically features a tower, a wrap-around porch, a gazebo, and windows of many shapes and sizes.

Also familiar to country dwellers are the *Gabeled Ell*, an L-shaped one- or two-story frame house, and the *Shotgun*, a long, narrow one-story house with the gabled end of the roof facing the road. You may also find a Vernacular Farmhouse, an informal, rambling two-story house with a one-story front porch and a combination of Colonial and Victorian features, as well as an *American Foursquare*, a massive, box-shaped two-story building with a hipped dormer and a deep, one-story porch. And,

> ### Saving Money on Heating Your Home
>
> Heating in the country can be expensive, especially when you're surrounded by harvested corn fields and there is nothing to keep the winter wind from getting a running jump before it slams into your house. Fortunately, there are things you can do to keep your costs down.
>
> Turning down the thermostat is the most obvious way to save money in heating your home. But that is merely *fuel* conservation, and it's hard to hear what Roseanne is snarling to Dan when your teeth are chattering. What really pays off in home heating is heat *conservation*, and there are several things you can do to help it along.
>
> Most home heat is lost through loose-fitting windows and doors, open chimney flues, stove and dryer vents, and other open avenues to the great outdoors. Caulking and weather-stripping materials can pay for themselves many times over. Storm windows and low-E glass also help. If windows are still drafty, you can always apply a clear plastic sealing, which is remarkably effective and costs only a few dollars.
>
> Since heat rises, attic insulation is another good way to conserve heat. Wall cavaties can be filled with blown-in cellulose.
>
> **The American Council for an Energy Efficient Economy** (1001 Connecticut Ave., NW, Suite 801, Washington, DC 20036) can send you a useful guide to other ways to conserve heat in your home.

of course, there are tens of thousands of country homes which fit into no architectural categories whatsoever.

If you don't like what is already on the market, you can always build. Skilled construction people—carpenters, roofers, bricklayers and the like—can be found almost everywhere. In the country, you don't have to worry quite so much about unreliable estimates or paying the so-called prevailing wage. You don't always need to pay an architect, either. Pre-fabricated houses are becoming increasingly popular because they are comfortable, easily assembled, and very reasonably priced (less than a third of the cost of conventionally built dwellings). You can also buy log cabin kits which range from the small Abe-Lincoln-slept-here type to huge two-story homes, with porches and your pick of everything else. Even mobile homes are becoming increasingly popular. No longer resembling the trailers of *Life* magazine fame, the new generation of mobile homes offer such comfortable and luxurious options as permanent foundations, built-in garages, and large, double-wide frames with no detectable seams.

No matter what you build or where you build it, zoning in the country is less than strict. Rural informality cushions—indeed, even frustrates—red tape obstructions such as overly restrictive building codes and conditions. This makes country construction about as close to hassle-free as you're going to get. That doesn't mean you can get away with everything. Even the most rural counties have inspectors and building codes. Especially with new houses, somebody's probably going to look it over and make sure everything is jake. But the prevailing attitude seems to be that, as long as what you build is safe, it's your land, and you can pretty much do what you want. And when it comes to putting up other, non-inhabited buildings—sheds, garages, outbuildings, etc.—or even remodels or additions...well, a lot of that often winds up overlooked. More often than not, it depends on where you are and what you're up to (and sometimes how well-liked you are by your neighbors), but you can generally count on proceeding without much official interference.

> **Checklist for Buying a Log Home**
>
> - Make sure you understand all terms and conditions of the purchase contract and warranty. See to it that all verbal promises have been included in writing.
> - Have the producer provide a list of whatever you will need (windows, roof shingles, etc.) to complete the home, with average market prices for each item.
> - Ask if logs will need to be cut at the job site, and whether holes are pre-drilled for spikes, bolts, or electrical wiring.
> - Calculate how much the delivery charges are per mile. Determine what equipment you'll need for unloading. Ask if the driver will help. Ask that the logs be covered during transport to keep them free of road dirt.
> - Ask what technical assistance the seller will provide. Ask who will be giving the assistance and what his or her qualifications are.

Making Sure The Doctor Is In

Another important factor you might want to consider is the local availability of health care. Everyone needs a little medical attention now and then, and you don't want to find out the hard way that getting needed health care in your new home town is a problem.

Not that it isn't already a problem for many Americans. The skyrocketing costs of medical care, coupled with exorbitant insurance rates and inadequate coverages, may well lead to a wholesale revamping of the entire national health system. In fact, it seems more than likely that the United States may be making a transition toward a universal health care plan. It's not such a revolutionary idea. After all, Harry Truman only advocated some sort of national health program more than forty years ago.

Despite the welcomed sanity that a national plan may introduce to overall health care, it won't affect the health care of rural Americans as quickly as it will benefit their city cousins. The fact remains that there just aren't enough caregivers to go around in the country. According to the U.S. Department of Health and Human Services, for example, there are 234 MDs for every 100,000 urbanites in the western states but only 115 doctors per 100,000 rural residents. Other areas are similar. In the Northeast, there are 284 urban doctors and 137 rural, while the comparable ratios are 230-to-89 in the South and 227-to-83 in the Midwest. At the same time, according to the American Hospital Association, 280 rural hospitals—one in seven—closed during the 1980s. Meanwhile, doctors and nurses continue to abandon rural areas in favor of metropolitan regions offering more lucrative practices.

All this statistical doom and gloom, however, doesn't change the basic fact that it is still possible to move to the Boondocks and enjoy the security of knowing that health care is close at hand. As with so much else in this country, it depends on where you choose to live. Blanket statements about the dwindling numbers of country doctors, nurses, and hospitals are oversimplifications relevant only to certain places, certain small towns. In reality, most rural areas still offer more than adequate health care, complete with well-trained country doctors, competent country nurses, and a sufficient number of country hospital beds.

In fact, things are actually looking up for medical treatment in rural America. The national health care crisis has spawned a number of health care initiatives with the expressed purpose of boosting health care availability for rural residents. Many medical schools now arrange for graduates to do part of their training in rural areas in the hopes of encouraging young doctors to settle in small towns. The National Health Services Corps has increased funding for migrant and community health centers. At the same time, Medicaid has been revamped to cover more pregnant women and to support comprehensive prenatal care.

The availability of health care is just one criterion in choosing a rural destination. Make sure you'll have convenient access to hospitals and emergency facilities. Find out who the local doctors are, how long they've been there, and what sort of reputations they enjoy with your prospective new neighbors. Consider your own health as well as your willingness and ability to drive to seek necessary medical attention. Health care may be a concern in small towns, just as it is elsewhere. If fast, easy access to medical treatment is a priority for you, your country haven probably still exists. Just be sure to look carefully and investigate thoroughly before you move.

Maybe You Could Use Some Professional Help

There are a number of ways to get help selecting the right rural area.

You might start by asking the federal government, a surprising source of information about rural living. One particularly useful service is offered by the ERS (Economic Research Service), which assigns every county in every state a "Beale Code" number summarizing its "population concentration." The Beale Code uses numbers from 0 to 9 to describe a county's urban/rural breakdown. Rural counties are those with Beale Codes of 6 or greater, according to the following definitions:

Beale Code 6: the largest city is smaller than 20,000, and the county is adjacent to a metropolitan area.

Beale Code 7: the largest city is smaller than 20,000, and the county is not adjacent to a metropolitan area.

Beale Code 8: a completely rural county which is adjacent to a metropolitan area.

Beale Code 9: a completely rural county which is not adjacent to a metropolitan area.

To help you identify the rural areas of the nation, Appendix A lists every rural county with a Beale Code of 6 or greater, alphabetically by state. Be aware, however, that Beale Codes do not necessarily correspond to the presence or absence of Boondocks. Just because Connecticut, New Jersey, and Rhode Island do not, by Beale code measure, contain any rural counties does not mean there are no rural areas within those states.

Another way is to take out a short-term subscription to the local newspaper of the area you have in mind. Boondock papers easily become lost in the more than 1,600 dailies in the United States. But the daily paper(s) of the nearest heavily-populated area will often contain some coverage of the less-inhabited neighborhoods in its region. You can find the names, addresses, phone/fax numbers, subscription costs, and special features of such papers in the *Editor & Publisher's International Yearbook*. Many library reference sections will also include a recent volume of *Newspaper Rates and Data*, published by the Standard Rate and Data Service of Wilmette, Illinois. This volume provides newspaper addresses as well as various population, income, and household statistics about the readers of individual papers. (Here's a useful tip: If you do subscribe to a local

> **Searching by Computer**
>
> Computer owners, take note: on-line databases can be remarkably useful sources of information about rural towns and areas. If you have access to the right databanks, you can find all sorts of information about states, regions, and localities, and learn a lot about a prospective home town from the census data and other collections of statistical facts that are available.
>
> If you belong to the data service, Compuserve, for example, you have access to a treasure chest of information in the "Demographics" database. The demographic reports available here will help you find out about the people who live in specific states, counties, and zip codes. One report classifies the populations of individual zip codes by age, occupation, income, and household size, among other characteristics. Other reports will give you information about regional civic activity, sports and recreational pastimes, and, to an amazing degree, even the personal interests of the inhabitants of individual zip codes.
>
> A word of caution, however. Try to narrow your search down to a few places before you log on and call up the demographic databases. The downloaded reports are not free, and asking for more than a few of them can put an appreciable dent in your moving budget.

paper, be sure to let the circulation department know that you want to receive the classified sections and shopping inserts. Otherwise, these may be left out to save postage.)

More helpful than a daily, though probably harder to get your hands on, would be the weekly newspaper that reports on your chosen country area. Small town weeklies, naturally enough, are apt to contain more of the specific information you're seeking and more likely to give you a better picture of life in the town or township you're considering. Your local library should have a list of the addresses and, sometimes, the phone numbers of such publications in your state, if not for the entire country. The *Newspaper Rate and Data* volume mentioned above will again provide you with useful numbers.

A call to ACCRA (the American Chamber of Commerce Researchers Association) might also be helpful. Every three months, ACCRA puts out a report on the costs of housing, food, services, transportation and health care for a "typical" family of four in 250 locations around the United States. Don't depend totally on these numbers. Like the metropolitan dailies, this survey concentrates on big city areas. Besides, your family may not be the "typical family of four" used as a model. Still, such information can be used to compare one part of the U.S. to another. This is more valuable than it may first appear, because you can often tell quite a bit about the rural areas surrounding a given city by finding something out about the city itself. The ACCRA offers a year's subscription of these quarterly surveys for $100, or you can have the latest quarter's survey sent to you for $50. Contact: **ACCRA, 1 Riverfront Plaza, Louisville, KY 40202, PH: (502) 566-5031.**

Once you know where you want to look, try calling the nearest Chamber of Commerce. If it belongs to ACCRA, it can and will give you a lot of the information you seek right over the telephone.

In the West, and especially in Southern California, where population density is becoming more and more of a problem, relocation to the country is an increasingly hot topic. In response, at least two relocation services have sprung up: the Greener Pastures Institute in Sierra Madre, California and *The Small Town Observer* in Bend, Oregon.

Bill Seavey, called "the guru of getting the hell out" and "an eco-minded entrepreneur" by Pasadena papers, operates the Greener Pastures Institute as an information clearinghouse. It offers bi-monthly seminars on relocation concerns such as job searching, real estate values, identifying and becoming acclimated to small town life, as well as periodic classes on general relocation strategies. The Institute also publishes the *Greener Pastures Gazette*, a small quarterly newsletter for the outward bound. According to its letterhead, the *Gazette* is "dedicated to the search for countryside Edens where the Good Life still exists" and "interested in 'repopulating' the American countryside." The *Gazette* offers lots of helpful tidbits and editorial opinion on a wide variety of relocation topics, ranging from survivalism to car insurance. It sells for $22 a year and is available from: **Greener Pastures Institute, P.O. Box 1122, Sierra Madre, CA 91025, PH: (818) 355-1670.**

In addition, GPI has the largest relocation library in the United States. If it doesn't have enough or the right kind of relocation information to satisfy you, it can probably direct you to the resource that will.

If you're thinking about relocating to the Northwest, Tom Evons' *The Small Town Observer* offers professional insight into the states of Washington, Oregon, and Idaho. A refugee from California's increasingly crowded San Diego County, Evons uses the experience he, his wife, and two children gained from their own relocation to help others who are seeking to escape the escalating population and complications of urban life.

The Small Town Observer ($24 a year) is a quarterly publication chock-filled with all sorts of information about specific rural locales. This professional newsletter contains both color and black-and-white photographs and in-depth, thought-provoking articles on rural trends and other aspects of the Northwest and other rural areas. Formerly published as the *Northwest Relocation News*, *The Observer* discusses the pros and cons of country living, partly through interviews with urban transplants, and provides information on housing costs, medical resources, and just about any other topics you can think of. *The Small Town Observer* provides prices and descriptions on various homes for sale, particularly in Washington, Oregon and Idaho. It also offers books, area guides, and audio-video tapes on relocation, rural life, and more. Subscriptions are available from: **The Small Town Observer, P.O. Box 324, Bend, OR 97709, PH: (800) 535-8853.**

Both *The Small Town Observer* and the Greener Pastures Institute have emphasized issues of interest to people who are relocating to the Western part of the country. But both have expanded their regional focus to help as many would-be migrants as possible. Even if your destination is another geographical locale, both are good sources of information about finding home and hearth in the countryside.

Finally, if you are anticipating a retirement in rural splendor, a monthly news organ, *The Retirement Letter*, may be especially helpful. Designed and written with older Americans in mind, this twenty-year-old publication includes articles on lifestyles and relocation alternatives, as well as pension fund information, advice on how to avoid bad investments, and other items of interest. Subscriptions are available for $49 a year by contacting: **The Retirement Letter, 7811 Montrose Rd., Potomac MD 20854, PH: (301) 340-2100.**

CHAPTER III

Drive Time

❖

*(Transportation and other ways of gettin'
from here to there)*

Oh, Henry

> *One thing you can set down as
> sure is that cities are doomed.*

Thus spake Henry Ford, during the early years of this century when famous people were so important that they never spoke, just spake. Ford, the shrewd and tight-fisted automotive industrialist and mass-production innovator, foresaw the advent of the modern highway system. He perceptively figured that better and faster automobiles than his were inevitable and that an ever-growing population behind the wheels of such automobiles would create an overwhelming demand for more and better highways. He further predicted that automobile travel would become so much faster and more convenient that people would no longer need to live close to work or shops (or, for that matter, close to each other). Hence he saw the seeds of destruction for city life and city living sown by every automobile that came off the assembly line.

Henry wound up a little left of center on some of his predictions, such as the one that the car of the future would be black. But he wasn't totally wrong concerning the future of auto travel. Faster, more innovative automobiles *were* developed. While the Model-T strained to hit fifty, a 1935 Ford could zip along at no less than seventy-five miles per hour. And improved roads *were* built to accommodate the growing populace and the increasing popularity and affordability of the new automobiles. By 1937 President Franklin Roosevelt had begun to explore the construction of a system of national superhighways. On October 1, 1940, the Pennsylvania Turnpike, a four-lane divided highway between Harrisburg and Pittsburgh, was opened to the public. "America's Dream Road," it was called, and the *New York Times* rhapsodized that the flight of birds was "scarcely more swift and effortless than that of the driver of the new superroad."

It wasn't until the 1950s that the highway system Henry Ford envisioned began to be realized. President Dwight D. Eisenhower, a former general, recalled the military value of highways during World War II. Mindful of the example of the German *Autobahn*, he began the development of America's national interstate highway system. We liked Ike, Ike liked roads, and roads we got. If he didn't do anything else, and some say he didn't, Ike did give us a badly-needed modern highway system.

All these roads didn't have quite the impact Ford thought they would. When he spoke of the automobile as a means for any American to "enjoy the Sunday drive" and to "take his family into God's great open spaces," he assumed that cars and highways would indelibly change the landscape. Once roads opened up quick and easy access to the country, most people would choose to live there, industry would follow, and cities as America knew them would begin to waste away. Ford was a little off on this one, too. Cities continued to grow and prosper, but Ford's great migration to the country failed to materialize.

People in the country, though, still benefited tremendously from the new highway system. The construction of roads between states, from city to city to city, required the routing of many four-lane highways and other main drags throughout the countryside. And the building of interstates and main roads meant that new attention had to be paid to secondary and dirt highways, the back roads and byways of the country, so that country folk could get to the big four-laners. Many secondary routes were upgraded and improved and many dirt roads were paved over.

So, Ford wasn't entirely off base. These improvements made rural travel easier and more convenient for everyone, from farmer to factory worker. Travel from the country to the city, and back again, took less time and less effort than ever before. People were now able to live in the country and commute rather easily to work in the city, which many did and still do.

One additional development would have caught Henry Ford with his hood open. The ease and convenience of travel on interstate highways has pushed the suburbs further out from the cities into what once, only a few years ago, were rural areas. Thanks to the interstates, many areas which used to be country have become at least partially urbanized. As a result, you may have to move farther from a metropolitan center in your search for a rural spot that will remain truly rural.

Take Me Home, Country Road

A few quick words about those back roads and byways.

The 3,000,000-plus miles of roads criss-crossing the rural U.S. are not all interstate highways. Living in the country means a fair amount of travel along secondary highways—those regular, paved, two-lane roads that wind and climb through the countryside and often seem a little on the narrow side—and sometimes along back roads, also two-laners and more often than not made from dirt and/or gravel.

Paved country roads are normally in pretty good condition. In contrast to city driving, there isn't a lot of stopping and starting in country travel, and, of course, there's less traffic, so highways hold up pretty well. For the most part, they're state and county routes, so if any potholes get too big you can generally count on the state or county coming along to fix it.

Back roads conditions are more dependent on the weather and the local township. You can expect them to be dry and dusty when it's hot and muddy when it's wet. And if they're in an area of heavy snowfall, they're usually the last to be tended by snowplows, regardless of the jurisdiction responsible for their maintenance.

Heat, dust, rain, mud, snow, and other conditions and complications are all less severe if the particular back road happens to be lined by trees. The shade keeps the dust down in the summer, while the trees themselves protect the road somewhat during the wet and snowy seasons. Also, the local "powers that be" will often *oil down* in the summer—that is, send out a truck to spread used and otherwise useless oil along the road in front of houses—as another way of keeping dust to a minimum.

The Car as God

There is one thing you have to have in the country. It may be superfluous to life in the city or even the suburbs, but it is what makes modern country life possible, not to mention convenient and enjoyable. It is the most important thing you'll ever own...the one possession you can't throw in on a deal with the Devil...the *sine qua non* of country life...the cow's udder, the horse's mane, the lamb's wool...the essential essential...

Well, you get the picture. It is *The Car*.

Living in the country means purposely choosing a location that is some distance from the undesirable and unwanted effects of overcrowded life. It also means living quite a ways from some of those people and places—hairdressers and hardware stores, boutiques and coffee houses, art galleries and concert halls—that you need or want to patronize on a regular basis. And, sometimes a country address puts considerable distance between you and your job. All of which means that country living involves a lot of travel which is often a bit too ambitious to undertake comfortably on foot or even by bicycle. And *that* means there are few things more vital to modern country life than The Car.

Not surprisingly, the average country couple, like the average city couple, normally has two cars. In the country, though, no matter who drives which, the cars are broken down into two categories—The Good Car and The Work Car.

The Good Car, also known as the "styling" car, is used for trips to the in-laws, vacations, dates, showing off, for pleasure jaunts where you feel like traveling in style, and even for going to work if you have a fancy enough job. The Good Car, whether a new car or simply a newer car, is often a country status symbol. It is usually, though not always, kept noticeably clean inside and out, because it is considered an indicator of just how well you are doing in your life and career. Who the main driver of the styling car is depends entirely on who works outside the home, who has to drive farthest to work—the closer the better for The Good Car, so as not to wear it out with too many miles—and who has the more professional position. (In those cases where both parties drive to white-collar jobs, two styling cars may be necessary.) Kids are kept out of the styling car whenever possible.

The Work Car, on the other hand, is usually a used and often an abused car. Also known as The Other Car, The Work Car is called into service for trips to the grocery store or shopping mall, for hauling the kids around, for driving to a blue-collar job, etc. For any trip or chore that means hard work or hard miles, The Work Car is the answer.

If you don't already own such cars, a move to the country means that you will probably have to acquire them. (A word to the wise: whether you are a couple or going it alone, if you have to get along with one car, make it The Work Car. It may not impress people as much, but you are going to need it far more often, and it is far more vital to country living.) Picking out a new or used car for rural use is a tad different than shopping for a city car, if only because The Car is much more crucial to the quality of rural life. The country car is in many ways a lifeline, a means of connection to services and conveniences and people you hold dear, and buying one calls for extra-careful consideration. It's not just the initial purchase, either. You also need to give some thought to the on-going care and maintenance which The Car is going to require.

Now, new cars are new cars and will have to be bought, city or country, from new car dealers. But not all new cars are equal. Since country living means more

Keeping Your Car From Looking Worked Over

The importance of keeping The Good Car looking good is obvious. Most country folk aren't quite as concerned with the appearance of the Work Car, so long as there isn't a huge hole in the floorboards and the doors don't fall off. Still, keeping The Work Car looking halfway decent can help it last longer and add to its eventual resale value.

Here are a few things to keep in mind about preserving the appearances of your Cars.

- Dents and scratches in you car retain moisture and lead to rust and corrosion. Simply adding plastic door strips, available at any automotive store, can save you from most dent damage. Small scratches can be hidden by rubbing with an ordinary wax crayon in a matching shade and buffing with a soft cloth.
- Road salt is another rust-causer. In winter, rinse your car at least once a week to prevent metal corrosion. Never use salt for traction when you get stuck in the snow. Cat litter works just as well, plus it absorbs odors and rust-causing moisture.
- Don't park under trees. In winter, falling icicles can put nasty dents in your car. In summer, tree sap and bird droppings can permanently discolor paint. (Remove sap and bird doo with a little cooking oil on a soft cloth; then rinse with warm water.)

travel, gas mileage is more important than ever. In addition, more use means more of certain types of maintenance. You don't want to wind up with some foreign job which local mechanics are less familiar with or which requires specially ordered or hard-to-get parts. It is also a down-to-country-earth reality that, in light of present trade imbalances, more than a few country folk consider purchasing a foreign car to be some sort of unpatriotic act. This is not to bad-mouth foreign cars.

But if you are concerned about the first impression you will make on your new country neighbors (and this is not something to ignore), a brand-new foreign car might be something of a liability.

When it comes to buying a used Work Car, there are a number of factors to keep in mind. First, be honest with yourself: do you know a great deal about the inner workings of an automobile? If not, you might think about taking someone who does along with you when you look for your used car. Find a reliable mechanic, pay them if you have to, and take them along with you on your search for The Work Car. This will help you make sure the shaft is in your car and not you.

The best way to find a suitable used car is the obvious one. Look in the car-for-sale ads in local newspapers, select some that seem to fit your price range and other requirements, and go look at them. Check the mileage. Examine the engine. Drive the car at least five miles so it has a chance to warm up thoroughly, run it at different speeds, and see how it handles on straightaways, around curves, and up hills. If your prospective Work Car has an automatic transmission, pay close attention to how it shifts. When you're done with the test drive, park the car on a clean, smooth surface, such as concrete, and look under the vehicle to see if anything is leaking.

(This approach has been called the kick-the-tire method. Literally kicking the tires won't tell you much, but if you still feel you have to kick them, go ahead. If your foot goes through to the rim, you may want to consider other prospects.)

Once you have purchased the vehicle(s) you want, you have to be concerned with upkeep. As with the car search, if you're not the Great Mechanic type, you'll need help in the care and feeding of your vehicle. Almost every rural area has some local establishment that

> ### Finding a Good Country Garage
> Finding a trustworthy place to get your flats fixed, your muffler muffled, or your engine energized is a must if you want to keep your car(s) in good running order. Especially in the country, even if you're a do-it-yourselfer, your vehicles are only as good and reliable as the mechanics who work on them.
>
> Even though there are laws and standards which mechanics must or should abide by, your best bet is to find a mechanic whom you know and can trust. This doesn't mean you have to have them over for Sunday dinner before you let them work on your car. Just ask around a little. In every rural area it seems that there's at least one local mechanic whom everybody swears by (instead of at.) If the people in the town you move to are satisfied with a certain garage, chances are you will be, too.

everyone knows is the best around. Find it. For non-mechanics, discovering a reliable mechanic and/or garage to watch over your car may be the most important single thing you can do to make sure your life in the country is enjoyable.

Why You Might Want To Pick Up a Pick-Up

For many country people, the best Work Car is a truck.

Specifically, a pick-up truck. No matter what the make or model (again, as long as it's American), pick-ups have many uses in the country. Depending on your lifestyle, you may even find that having a truck around will save you a lot of time, trouble and, in some cases, money.

You can use your pick-up to haul everything from a week's groceries to entire Little League teams quickly and conveniently. Trucks move more easily through and over rough terrain or flooded roads, both of which are not unusual in the country. And if you adopt the farming life, you may find yourself rushing a sick calf to the vet, taking a litter of pigs to the market, or transporting bushels of sweet corn to the nearest corner for fun and profit.

Even if you aren't into farming, potential country uses for pick-ups crop up all the time. Coming home with the annual Christmas tree. Hauling trash to the nearest landfill or recycling center. Taking the TV in for repairs. Buying, selling, and delivering chairs, pianos, riding lawnmowers, refrigerators, or a thousand and one other bulky items. Bringing bags of salt for the water conditioner. Lugging work tools, spare tires, fishing tackle, camping gear, snowmobiles, motorcycles, bicycles, and almost anything else.

Locating a suitable model of this country workhorse calls for the same careful consideration you'd give to finding a Work Car. And again, if you don't know a lot about trucks, find someone who does to help you locate a good bargain. You don't *have* to own a pick-up to live in the country. Many people live there for years without owning one or wanting to. But pick-ups do come in awfully handy in rural areas. After all, hauling a fragrant load of manure in your Chevette can get a little awkward and more than a little messy. Especially if the Chevette is The Good Car.

Let's Be Careful Out There

Statistically speaking, one of the few areas where country life is more hazardous than city life is on the road.

It stands to reason. Except for the bottlenecks caused by road construction and wrecks or the natural disasters that block traffic flow, slow, bumper-to-bumper traffic is scarcely known in the country. What *is* known are wide-open spaces, long stretches of open road, and scarcities of encumbering traffic and spoilsport police. As a result, traveling by car in rural areas generally

> ### Cover Your Pickup Truck Safely
>
> A recent study in the *Journal of the American Medical Association* concluded that anyone, kids or adults, riding in the back of covered pickup trucks may be in danger of carbon monoxide poisoning.
>
> Of 68 children sent to a Virgina medical center for accidental carbon monoxide poisoning from 1985 to 1991, 20 had been passengers in the back of pickup trucks with hard shells or tarpaulin covers. Fifteen of the twenty were knocked out by fumes. One later died, and another suffered permanent brain damage.
>
> The trucks involved were not campers, but covered pickups with exhaust pipes or leaks that vented fumes toward the back instead of the sides.

means higher speeds, and these higher speeds result in more serious accidents in the country than in metropolitan areas. In 1990, the National Highway Safety Traffic Administration reported 22,340 fatal crashes in rural areas, compared to only 17,287 in urban locales. Moreover, half of the fatal crashes occurred at speeds of 55 miles per hour or greater, with a higher proportion of these (71.4%) occurring on rural roads than on urban streets (21.5%).

It makes sense to be extra-careful when you're behind the wheel in the country. Though most roads are paved, they're also usually a good bit narrower than freeways. What with curves and hills and oncoming traffic, as well as cross traffic from driveways and sideroads, they're not intended for high-speed travel. Moreover, instead of a grassy median strip or a guardrail, what you'll find waiting beside most country highways are ditches, rocks, trees, telephone poles, and other hazardous, generally immovable objects that are no fun at all to ram into. Drive time might be an especially good time to experience the country's slower pace. Wherever you're going will be there when you get there. And, as everywhere, no matter how fast or slow you're traveling, wearing a seat belt on rural roads is a sensible precaution for driver and passenger alike.

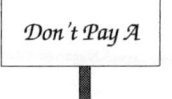

Winter travel is particularly demanding in the country. Snow and ice, even on paved roads, are significant limiting factors. Going slowly and carefully is even more important than ever. So is making sure that your car is winterized with antifreeze, snow tires, and the like, and in good running order. Experienced country drivers learn to keep plenty of gas in the tank to ward off possible fuel line freeze-up. None of this prevents car trouble, so stashing the phone number of the nearest reliable, all-night tow truck service somewhere in your vehicle is a good idea. Especially at night, you can wait quite a while for another car to come to your rescue.

If you don't have a phone in your car or truck—and even if you do—installing a CB radio might be a better idea. You never know just where in the country you might break down, and it could well be quite a ways from the nearest phone. A CB will allow you to contact help immediately. It can, quite literally, be a life-saver in those situations where every minute counts.

Whether winter or summer, just knowing the local roads can add to your margin of safety. Slow down when you know there's a hill or a curve coming up. Country traffic can include tractors and other self-propelled farm implements, horses, buggies, bicycles, and all manner of slow-moving vehicles. Watching out for the other guy is always important, and never more so than when the other guy is just around the bend, driving fourteen thousand pounds of John Deere combine at 15 miles per hour in your lane.

Crossing train tracks in rural areas is another occasion that often calls for an extra measure of caution.

Clearing the Winter Driveway

If you settle on a place where Jack Frost nips at nasal hairs during part of the year, you will have to participate in the annual battle of keeping your driveway free from snow. In parts of the country driveways can be long and gravelly. Getting down one of these drives when the snow is "as high as an elephant's eye" can be a big problem.

You can't exactly use your snowblower in your new country drive. A long driveway takes a surprisingly long time to blow snow out of. Besides, snowblowers have nasty habits of depositing half your gravel driveway into your yard and bouncing rocks off your spouse's forehead. Not wise.

You can shovel the drive by hand, but that makes for an even longer day than a snowblower and a sore back to boot. You can keep plenty of sand or cat litter on hand and hope that they will give you enough traction to bulldoze your old Chevy all the way to the road. Chances are you'll get stuck at least once, though, and revving your engine to ten-grand as you try to rock your vehicle out of a snow-filled rut isn't exactly recommended by your manual. Swearing until you're red in the face isn't exactly recommended by your doctor.

So, if you don't own your own snowplow or tractor with a snowblade attached, the best thing to do is what I do. Call my cousin Dennis. He owns a truck with a snowblade.

Most country track crossings have flashing lights, descending bars, and the whole bit—but not all of them. Some are just flashing lights, and others aren't anything more than wooden signposts which read *Railroad Crossing*. In all cases, no one should need to be told to stop and look both ways before crossing.

Other Ways of Getting Around

As elsewhere, there are other ways to get around in the country besides cars and trucks. One of the most popular is walking.

That may seem strange, since, as noted, there's often quite a distance between country home and destination. But it's possible to live in the country, and still be within walking distance—which is however long you say it is—of your neighbors, the grocery store, a restaurant, or a post office. It is not unusual for children to walk to and from school, especially if school is no more than a mile or so away. And country residents of all ages can enjoy the health benefits that walking has been shown to provide. If nothing else, striding along in the fresh air and open spaces of the country certainly beats hotfooting it around the shopping mall.

Bicycling is another popular means of getting around in the country. Country roads are often narrow, so prudence dictates that cyclists stop or at least pull over to the shoulder or grass beside the road when motorized traffic approaches. Put simply, most country highways were not designed to include both cars and bicycles. Safety and common sense both dictate that motorized traffic be given as wide a berth as possible regardless of who has the legal right of way.

Motorcycles are often seen—and heard—roaring through the country. While it's true that some local laws don't require helmets—and even if they do, many people don't bother wearing them—it seems, as with seat belts, only sensible to do all you can to keep safe. Helmet or not, though, zooming through the countryside astride a motorcycle is one of the more exhilarating ways to get where you're going. With far less traffic, far fewer stops-and-starts, and far more open road, the country often allows for miles of uninterrupted cycling.

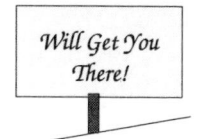

Riding a horse is also pretty big fun, even if you've never wanted to be Victoria Barkley or Little Joe Cartwright. In many rural areas, travel by horse is not unusual. Hitching posts are common sights, as are harness shops that sell "tack"—saddles, bridles and the like—for use on Old Paint or Triggerless. Wherever you live, however, owning a horse is a big responsibility. Horses, like people, eat every day, and that means there's another little task known as "stall cleaning." You may want to find out more about this before deciding to become the next Lone Ranger.

Whether you're travelling via bicycle, motorcycle, horse, foot, or thumb, the country offers a wonderful panorama of unique sights, sounds, and smells. This is not to recommend gawking while operating any sort of vehicle, but the country traveller regularly passes forests and farmlands, rushing rivers and rolling prairies, crystal-clear lakes and streams, and many other natural, scenic landmarks. Burma Shave signs have, regrettably, faded from the landscape, but there are many other man-made wonders to marvel at along the way, such as picturesque farmhouses or big barns and silos that look as though they've grown right out of the earth. You can also hear the musical calls of birds, the lowing of cattle, or the chirping of crickets. Take a deep breath. That's new-mown hay you're smelling.

It's enough to make you wonder how subways have survived.

Planes, Trains, Buses and Taxis

Rural dwellers aren't likely to live close to airports or train depots or have bus stops or taxi stands at the nearest corner. Almost always The Car is used to take little Hermie to the train station or to meet Uncle Dreeb's plane. That's not necessarily an inconvenience.

Depending on where you live, the airport or train station may not be that far away. And, like other rural trips, most of the mileage will be through an uncongested countryside, where ten miles may only take ten minutes. So even if you're twenty miles or so from the nearest airport or train depot, you're really a lot closer than it sounds.

As for buses, they're more of a city convenience. There may be some kind of county bus system, but the typical small town or village is not going to have or even need a bus line for everyday travel. (For longer trips, though, you can usually find an inter-regional bus depot within reasonable driving distance.)

Taxis, too, are urban phenomena, except in selected rural areas. In parts of the Midwest, for example, noticeable portions of the population are Amish, who reject automobile ownership. In these areas, some people actually make a living "hauling Amish," usually by vans though sometimes in cars, and charging so much per mile. (The Amish may not believe in owning cars, but they recognize the realities forced upon them by modern society. Most of them have no objection to *riding* in motorized vehicles and paying for the service.) Though such "taxi services" are normally used only by the Amish, anybody can hire them, and they can be extremely handy for anyone without access to a car.

It all comes back to The Car again. The fact is that, despite all the other means of local travel, if you don't like to drive a car, you should be extremely careful about where you locate in the country. You can still move to a rural area, of course. But make sure you are close enough to town to walk or bicycle to the store, the post office, the bank, or wherever. Fortunately, you can still do that and enjoy the benefits of a rural lifestyle in a rural setting.

CHAPTER IV

MoneyMoneyMoneyMoney

❖

(Making bucks in the boondocks)

How's The Job Going?

You don't need to look any further than current headlines to know that employment in the good old USA can seem pretty bleak at times. That's just as true for the average country Joes and Josephines looking for farm work or industrial jobs as it is for the misplaced stockbrokers and former secretaries pounding the pavements of our cities. Sometimes it seems as if everyone in the country is out of a job or expecting to be. Sad to say, some of the reasons people give for considering a move to the country include the loss of an urban job, uncertainty about continued employment, and concern about being able to keep on making urban mortgage payments while still paying other bills.

It's also true that rural workers haven't fared any better than their urban counterparts. Most haven't even done as well. Recent figures show rural rates of unemployment to be anywhere from 3 to 5 per cent higher than urban rates. Or more. Non-metropolitan employment has lagged behind city and suburban employment for some time. Between 1979 and 1986, for example, rural employment rose by only 5.7 per cent while metropolitan employment climbed some 15 per cent.

It is not just the current (1990-1992) recession that has been responsible. The United States has been shifting from an economy built around industries which produce goods to one based on firms which deliver services. Meanwhile, American companies have been challenged by increased amounts of global competition. Technology has replaced labor, costs have been trimmed, workers have been laid off, and new jobs have not been created. During the last decade, job growth has slowed in all parts of the country, but recent economic changes have hit rural workers especially hard.

So does all this mean you'll have a harder time making a living in the country than elsewhere? Nope, not necessarily. For one thing, the overall employment picture might not be as depressing as it seems. Even though a lot of people have been thrown out of work or accepted work with lower pay and benefits, the fact remains that a vast majority of Americans are still working. Moreover, the Department of Labor projects that, though some industries will permanently lose jobs, some 18 million new jobs will be added to the U.S. economy by the year 2000.

But job statistics don't tell all the story. Just because you live in the country does not mean you have to work there. In fact, residing in a rural area while commuting to a city job is still a very popular, very viable arrangement. Some people don't even have to commute. Recent technological developments have opened the door to *telecommuting*, allowing many country residents to hold down city jobs without ever leaving the country. Home-based businesses are also on the rise, as are new business start-ups of all kind, at least according to Dun &

Bradstreet, which reported that 1.3 million new enterprises were started in 1990 alone.

Your chances of moving to the country and finding ways to put pasta on the table and tapes in the Nintendo may be better than you think. Depending on individual considerations such as your educational background, your personal and interpersonal skills, your current financial condition, and your abilities to adapt and persist, your employment prospect may actually be enhanced in the country, where individual gumption is not overwhelmed by sheer weight of numbers.

It doesn't matter whether you're thinking about the country as a field of new professional opportunities or a gateway to a new, country lifestyle. There are a large number of employment alternatives for you to choose "out where the green grass grows."

Make Less, Gain More

You may be concerned that a move to the country will mean a reduction in your income. This isn't necessarily so. For one thing, as we shall see, you might not even have to change jobs. But even if you can't take your job with you, and even if your new country job does result in a smaller paycheck, the lower overall costs of country living could actually leave you with more in the bank.

In a recent article on the advantages of small-town life, *Kiplinger's Magazine* told about Liz and Henry Bothfeld and their three children. Fed up with overwhelming traffic and crime problems, the Bothfelds gave up on their suburban Chicago hometown and moved to a small town in Wisconsin. Both were fully prepared to sacrifice some income to gain the advantages of country life. But they were in for a surprise.

First, they found that could sell their 4-bedroom suburban home for $236,000 and buy a 4-bedroom rural home, with lots more room for themselves and their children, for $63,000. Their monthly mortgage payments dropped from $1,000 to $320. And the extra bucks in the bank were only the beginning.

Henry expected to continue working as a self-employed electronic-marketing consultant, commuting and telecommuting to clients in the big city. Instead, he found an unexpected opening with a local employer. Technically, his new job pays less. But now he pockets the $4,000 a year that he previously spent on health insurance when he was self-employed.

The Bothfelds also benefit from the significantly lower costs of child care. In Chicago, an in-home babysitter charged some $5.00 an hour. In small-town Wisconsin, the Bothfeld children are cared for by a neighbor who runs a state-licensed day care home. The total cost of day care for all three offspring is now $3.00 an hour. And where the Bothfelds used to have trouble finding an evening babysitter at any price, they've discovered that their new home town is filled with plenty of teenage babysitters who consider $1.50 an hour to be a reasonable wage.

The Bothfeld's case is not unusual. Book publicist Lucinda Dyer fled overpopulated Los Angeles—she thinks it may have been the day more people were killed in L.A. than in Beirut—for the countryside of Tennessee and changed careers from publicizing other peoples' books to writing her own. If her net income dipped slightly, her expenses plunged dramatically. She traded her $1,200-a-month urban rent for a $785 monthly mortgage on a two-story home. Her car insurance premiums are $1,000 a year less, and even her medical insurance premiums are lower than when she lived in the city. In her words, "it just costs less to live here."

Your own profession, abilities, and the opportunities available to you in the area where you settle will determine exactly how much money you can expect to make and to pocket. But, contrary to much popular wisdom, moving to the country does not mean you'll earn less money. You might even earn more. And even if you do end up making less than you made in the city, the lower costs of country living may actually give you a higher standard of living than you had before your move.

Farm Living

Writer S.J. Perlman once said a farm was nothing more than "an irregular patch of nettles, bound by short-term notes, containing a fool and his wife who didn't know enough to stay in the city."

No getting around it. Urban life makes some people downright bitter.

The surprising truth is that only about one country resident in twelve actually lives on a farm. Not only is there a variety of alternative employment opportunities in the country, but, to be honest, farming is not exactly the fast lane to financial independence. If it were, we wouldn't need Farm Aid concerts, and the farmer and wife in Grant Wood's well-known *American Gothic* would be grinning from ear to ear.

Unless you plan to purchase a very successful, working farm, expecting to move to the country and start right in living off the land isn't realistic. Many experienced farmers can't even manage that. If you intend to farm, be prepared to begin on a part-time basis. And don't expect instant gratification. Farming, whether part-time or full, calls for years of hard-earned know-how to produce successful results. The best advice for a beginner is to start small and work up. Don't go out and plow up a hundred acres, planting and harvesting and all that, until you develop a feel for the farming life. Read as much as you can about farming. Your local library should have a fair collection of magazines and books on farms and farming. Familiarize yourself with local weather patterns and other conditions. Talk to your neighbors—if you don't make a pest of yourself, they can and probably will tell you about local conditions, planting strategies, and the like. Do everything you can to prepare for running your farm, then ease into it. This will help you keep your shirt while you learn how to earn on a farm.

You will also need to give some thought to what kind of farming you want to pursue. Like urologists and field-goal kickers, many farmers have become specialists of sorts. There's crop farming, which concentrates on raising wheat, hay, or other types of cash crops and selling them at market. There's livestock farming, in which would-be Old and Young McDonalds raise cows, pigs, sheep, chickens, etc., selling some off each year and keeping the rest for breeding and an occasional Sunday dinner. There's also dairy farming, where you depend on milk cows to provide a monthly milk check and the cows depend on you for everything else.

Another alternative is custom farming, where you don't need to farm your own land at all. You simply rent out your equipment—and yourself as operator—to other, less well-equipped farmers. Suppose Farmer Jones has two-hundred acres of wheat needing to be cut and threshed. Say a mechanical breakdown, a bad streak at the gaming table, or a shortage of investment funds has left him without access to a combine. You, Farmer Ex-cityboy, drive in with your combine, help harvest the wheat, and split the money with Farmer Jones. (It gets even better. Most custom farmers normally hire themselves out as their own equipment operators instead of letting the Farmer Joneses of the world operate it. Chances are no one will take as good care of your equipment as you will. Besides, your fees as equipment operator are on top of what you earn from your share of the harvest.)

These and other methods of farming all have their own unique advantages. Managed carefully, they all can be more or less profitable. But again, keep your expectations reasonable. Don't expect to make a big killing as a beginner—most long-time farmers have enough trouble turning a profit—and don't try to move to the country and make a switch to full-time farming all in one humongous bite. Start slowly and adapt, gradually increasing your farming activities as you gain knowledge and experience. You'll stand a much better chance of finding success as a farmer.

Also be prepared to supplement your farm income with non-farm earnings. Off-farm income includes more than wages and salaries from nonfarm jobs. It also includes nonfarm business income, rent from nonfarm real estate, dividends, interest, social security checks, pensions and many other earnings that can, and do, contribute to a farmer's financial well-being. To be frank, growing numbers of farmers have had to depend on off-farm income to live the good life. In 1973, forty per cent of the farm population's personal income came from nonfarm sources. By 1982, that percentage had risen to sixty, and indications are that it's even higher in 1992. So, do think long and hard before pulling on those coveralls.

Non-Farmers in the Dell

The majority of our sixty-three million-plus country dwellers, those whom the government refers to as "rural non-farm residents," are...well, rural non-farmers. That is, they may live in the country, with country house, lots of elbow room, and all the other rural perks, but they aren't dependent on making a living or even pulling in a partial income from the land.

Moving to the country doesn't mean you have to contract for forty acres and a mule. The farming life can be great. Many people dream about moving back to the land, tilling the soil and all that, and some of them actually will. But you don't have to. The simple fact is that most people who live in the country choose *not* to be farmers.

How Blue Is Your Collar?

The fact that blue-collar jobs, especially in manufacturing, are being affected by such factors as the shift to a service economy does not mean that this type of work is threatened. To the contrary, in many rural areas, certain types of working jobs are actually on the rise. So if you're looking for hands-on employment in agriculture, in construction, or in some other, traditionally blue-collar field, your prospects in the country will be no worse, and may actually be better, than they are in many of our cities.

Take manufacturing. While the decline in manufacturing jobs is well documented and probably not reversible, a few areas are experiencing real growth. Plastics workers, for example, will benefit from the increasing substitution of plastic for metal in many products. Meanwhile, expansion in the printing and publishing industries will sustain job growth for laborers in those areas, as well.

Construction jobs are basically seasonal, and construction work is sensitive to fluctuations in the economy. Nevertheless, the Department of Labor projects increases in the construction of households and industrial plants as well as rising demands for maintenance and repair of highways, dams, and bridges, all of which will stimulate an increase in construction activities. Carpenters, drywall workers, lathers, and all other construction workers can expect to find at least as much opportunity for employment in the country as they can in the city.

Automotive body repair is also experiencing faster-than-average growth as a result of increases in the number of vehicles on the road, the popularity of lighter weight cars (which are more easily damaged in collisions), and the greater difficulty of repairing today's body styles. In view of the vital roles cars and other vehicles play in country life, auto body repair promises to be an especially viable country career. For the same reason, there will also be an on-going need for mechanics and other auto-related professionals.

This is just a sampler. Every farm needs farmhands, every school needs janitors, every post office needs mail carriers. Welders, electricians, plumbers, air conditioning and furnace repairers, truck drivers, tree trimmers, landscape laborers—every type of blue-collar worker is working in rural areas throughout the nation. Pay scales may vary, as may the local demand for specific blue-collar laborers. But if working with your hands or your back is your "bag," you'll find plenty of opportunities in the right country town.

Working From Home: It Don't Get No Better Than This

For many people the best, and certainly the most convenient, method of making money in the country involves working out of their homes. This may include telecommuting, telemarketing, industrial home work, sales, free-lancing, and starting your own home-based business.

Besides the obvious convenience of a fifteen-second commute down the hallway to your office, working at home offers a number of other benefits. Your work-related expenditures on car maintenance, gas, tolls, parking, bus fare, and other transportation expenses drop to near zero. You don't have to worry about your office wardrobe or work clothes, so your costs of clothing, dry cleaning, and laundry will drop significantly. You'll save money on lunch, too, since it's much cheaper to eat at home than to eat out when away on the job.

There are also a number of tax advantages to be gained from working at home. Offices in the home are business expenses and deductible on federal and most state income tax forms as long as you have a legitimate work space devoted exclusively to your business. You can't just work from the dining room table, call it your work space, and expect to get the Home Office Deduction. Home office expenses are deductible in proportion to the total square footage of your work space. You'll be able to deduct part of your rent or mortgage payment; part of your phone, electric, and gas bills; all of your equipment, supply, and material expenses; and all mileage driven for your business. You can also deduct postage, printing, photocopying, and eighty per cent of all business meals. In the case of home businesses, additional deductions may include advertising, bookkeeping, some of your vacation expenses, books, trade publications and seminars related to your work, insurance premiums, and even certain types of business-related entertainment.

It might even be possible to keep your current job even if you move to a rural location too far to commute more than occasionally. If you are temperamentally suited to such an arrangement, many jobs can be converted to "home work." If your employer is receptive to a creative solution like home work, you can have your job and your rural home, too.

It's not such an outlandish idea. Home work can benefit both business and employee, so you're not exactly asking for any favors when you propose changing your working arrangement. In fact, you might remind your employer of the twenty-per-cent increase in productivity that has typically resulted from switching an on-location job to home work. For many companies the costs of insurance, utilities, and maintenance, as well as the indirect expense of keeping investment capital tied up in additional office space, generally drop with each worker who operates from home. Finally, because home workers can be much more flexible in their schedules and because they are able to work even when a bit under the weather, absenteeism causes much less work disruption and other costly inconveniences.

Telecommuting for Fun and Profit

Describing "the new electronic heartland" in *Megatrends 2000*, John Naisbitt emphasizes that "...if cities did not exist, it now would not be necessary to invent them."

Naisbitt points out that personal computers, modems, fax machines, cellular phones, pagers, and other electronic marvels are revolutionizing the workplace, enabling people to work from home and liberating workers from the need to live close to work. He calls these the tools of telecommuting, an emerging technology which will certainly facilitate home work and offer lots of encouragement for anyone contemplating a move to the country.

Anyone who depends on a computer at work is an excellent candidate for telecommuting. Examples of telecommuting positions include typesetting, word processing, researching, transcribing, graphic designing, writing of all kinds, and any other service that can be performed through the use of computers and/or computer-related equipment such as faxes and modems. These jobs are really just the tip of the iceberg, though. Anyone capable of operating the tools of the electronic heartland is well-positioned to make a living without ever setting foot outside the door.

Better Living Through Sales

If you can't get your present employer to consider your telecommuting proposal, or if your present position simply doesn't permit a telecommuting arrangement, you may have to change employers or even careers when you move to the country. Many people have successfully turned to sales. Whether you're working for yourself or for someone else, a position in sales is a proven way to earn an income while retaining the basic advantages of home-based employment.

Telemarketing, or phone sales, is one of the most popular and convenient ways to earn money in sales. All you need is a good voice, a pleasant and persuasive manner, persistence and, of course, a phone or two. Telemarketing jobs are frequently listed in the "Help Wanted" sections of local newspapers. Even though telemarketing is usually a part-time activity, you can still make good money if you're paid on commission, and you still retain all the cost-saving advantage of working from home.

Maybe you don't feel that phone sales is right for you. Another form of telemarketing involves using your phone to invite prospective customers to demonstrations or home parties for displaying various products under comfortable conditions which are favorable for sales. The Fuller Brush Company and Avon Products,

Inc., once both identified almost exclusively with door-to-door sales, are only two examples of companies that now do most of their selling through telemarketing. There are many other companies looking for sales representatives who can be successful in this type of business.

Other companies are always looking for people who excel at person-to-person sales. One-on-one selling may involve some travel—usually by automobile—but what you lose in convenience may be made up in the healthy income potential of successful sales specialists. While you may have to visit the office on occasion, you can still retain a generous measure of independence and schedule flexibility without sacrificing the advantages of your home office. Good sales people are needed by many firms, including include insurance agencies, pharmaceutical corporations, and water softener equipment manufacturers, among many others.

Finally, if you'd prefer to stay away from phone calls *and* home visits and let the customers come to you, you can always look for a job in a retail outlet, such as a department store, or in automobile or appliance sales. You'll need to travel to these jobs, of course, but stores and car lots are everywhere, and, especially if you have prior sales experience, you should be able to find ample opportunities relatively close to your country home.

The Freedom of Free-Lancing

Whether you're working as a telecommuter or in a more traditional on-site location, the advantage of free-lancing is just what the term implies: freedom. You do depend on companies and individuals to "rent" your services, but you're basically your own boss, free to set your own hours and work at your own pace. It's not unlimited freedom. You do have to satisfy the needs and meet the deadlines of your clients in order to stay in

> **Multi-Level Marketing (MLM)**
>
> Many Fortune 500 companies, including Tupperware, Amway, and Mary Kay Cosmetics, now use multilevel marketing, or "network marketing," to sell their products. Though most people get involved in MLM to supplement their regular paycheck or help with the mortage, many make good money by becoming successful independent distributors. About 80 percent of MLM distributors are women.
>
> There's no guarantee of success, but payoffs can be substantial. Most MLM companies not only pay distributors commissions on sales, they offer bonuses—everything from toasters to new cars and paid vacations for those who attain certain levels of sales or recruitment.
>
> You don't have to risk a lot to see if it's for you, either. You can usually begin in MLM for a few hundred dollars or less. You can set your own schedule and work at your own pace. How successful you become depends to a great extent on your own efforts, your sales ability, and your persistence.
>
> Avon calling?

demand. But if you'd rather not keep regular hours or be forced to attend the company picnic, and if you're confident that your skills will keep you in steady work, then free-lancing may be for you.

On-site free-lance work remains the norm, at least for newcomers to the free-lance field. Some employers like to keep an eye on you, especially if you don't have much of a track record or if you've never done any work for them before. As with some sales jobs, free-lancers seeking on-site work will need to live in a rural area close enough to those employers—ad agencies, newspapers, and the like—who can and will use their services. But as your clients gain confidence in your ability and dependability you may be able to do more and more of your work from home, visiting the client only to pick up or drop off assignments. This type of free-lance work is particularly suited to photographers, calligraphers, commercial artists, and others whose skills are not bound to a fixed location.

Telecommuting can cut the expense and time invested in on-site visits to almost nothing. If you don't already have them, you may need to purchase the telecommuter's tools—a computer, a fax, a modem, etc.—but free-lancing may be an ideal solution for professionals like graphic artists, writers, editors, and others whose skills do not require an office environment.

Be forewarned, however. Successful free-lancing wherever it is practiced takes a lot of self-motivation. You've got to hustle if you're going to make a go of it, and there's usually no one there except yourself and your family to push or pull you to do your best work. If you prefer paid vacations and long lunch-breaks or need the helping hand (or foot) of a boss in order to get the best out of yourself, you may find life as a free-lancer to be a bit of a stretch.

The Voyages of the Entrepreneurship Enterprise

Like free-lancing, starting your own business takes loads of get-up-and-go, but it promises even greater freedom from the yoke of corporate tyranny (or whatever you want to call working for someone else). One of the main differences is that the home entrepreneur enjoys a number of potential rewards, such as keeping all the profits and running the whole show, that are never experienced by the average free-lancer. Being your own boss also means shouldering responsibilities, like paying advertising costs and raising investment capital, that the average free-lancer never has to worry about. If the potential payoff and personal satisfaction of running your own business is large, so is the risk: fifty per cent of home-based businesses fail within the first five years. Moreover, seventy-nine per cent of small-business owners put in over forty hours a week, fifty-three per cent work more as an owner than they ever did as an employee, and forty per cent never take a vacation longer than one week a year. This home-business stuff is not for the faint-hearted.

Nevertheless, if you have the kind of business experience or knowledge that can be transferred to a home business and if you possess a deep well of persistence and a dogged determination to succeed, you might give some thought to becoming your own boss. Despite the risks and uncertainties, if you are able to make a living from your very own business, right from your very own home, you can set up shop anywhere you wish.

Up to now, you may never have thought that your job experience could be parlayed into your own business when you relocated to your rural haven. A little imagination, however, opens up a world of possibilities. How hard would it be for a city sanitation worker, for example, to start a trash collection service in the country? For a business executive to establish a home-based consulting service? For a homemaker to begin a home cleaning business? Or an advertising copywriter to set up a writing services company? No matter what your urban job, look to see if you can turn it into a home-based business which allows you to enjoy the benefits of country life while still working at something you do well.

Using your present job skills as the cornerstone of a home business is only one option. Maybe you're an accountant who happens to be skilled in arts and crafts or a bus driver who has always wanted to operate your own mail order business. Your move to the country might also be your chance to try out something you've always wanted to do. Listen to your heart as well as your head in choosing a home business you can enjoy while you are making it work.

Don't expect to strike it rich right away. Especially during the first year, a new business normally means a lot of hours and usually not a whole lot of return. Make sure you have the financial wherewithal and the patience to build a successful business venture before declaring yourself president, CEO and all-around top dog of your very own enterprise.

Running a home-business can be very rewarding, both personally and financially. Many a mover and shaker has gotten started in just this way. Plus if you think that the president of your own company isn't making enough money, you can always give yourself a raise.

The Long and Winding Road

But, say you move to the country, keeping your present job or getting another one that does not allow for telecommuting, telemarketing, sales, free-lancing, or operating out of your home. Perhaps you decide to open your own business outside of your home. Or maybe you just don't want to—or can't—work from home.

Well, my friend, you'll need a little traveling music.

Country dwellers commuting to a city job are probably a lot more common than you might realize. You, too, may end up becoming a country commuter. If so, you'll be doing a good deal of driving, and one of the most important things you can do to make your working life as pleasant as possible is to make your commute as pleasant as possible.

As we have seen, convenient access to freeways and four-laners is the rule rather than the exception, and five miles of country road can often be driven faster than five blocks of city traffic. Remember, though, that you're

> ## Mail Order
>
> Mail-order has become an increasingly popular form of home business. All you need is an appealing product or products and a target audience and a way to reach it, and you're in business.
>
> Most experts say niche marketing—i.e., offering specialized products to a limited segment of people—is the wave of the mail order future. Experienced professionals and others in the know recommend a target market with a minimum of 250,000 prospective customers, because you'll need to develop a customer base large enough to keep your business thriving.
>
> Publishing and mailing your own catalog is the most expensive method, though you do get to keep more of the profits that way. Try to have your catalog reflect the unique identity of the products you're offering so that it will stand out from the pack.
>
> Getting your products on the pages of another company's catalog is a less expensive means of reaching customers and may be a better way to start out. Send a letter to the company with the catalog, including a picture or a sample of your product. In the letter describe your product's advantages and explain why it fits with that company's product offerings.
>
> The Direct Marketing Association estimates that 54.4 per cent of American adults purchased products through mail order in 1990. And in 1991, consumer and businesses spent an estimated $175.1 billion on mail order products. There's no reason why some of that money couldn't be sent to *your* mail order business.

going to be making this drive every working day. Make certain that there's a convenient, well-maintained route to your job before you close the deal on your country estate. Try to map out an easy route, one with few stops, good roads, and pleasant driving conditions. It also helps if your city job isn't in a huge metropolis. While you aren't likely to have any country traffic problems, you will naturally begin to experience more congestion as you near your urban job site. Fortunately, even during rush hour, smaller cities usually don't have nearly the traffic problems of Los Angeles, New York, or Chicago.

Whether you commute long distances or simply run business errands, the car is as central to work as it is to the rest of country life. Make your vehicle as comfortable as possible. Not so comfortable that you fall asleep and take a header into the nearest guardrail, but comfortable enough to make driving restful as opposed to rigorous. Adjust your seat so that you're not too close or too far away from the steering wheel (this seems obvious, but a surprising number of people don't think to do it). Your back will thank you. Maybe even keep a few munchies on hand, preferably something with a long shelf life like peanuts or hard candy that won't melt all over the road map in your glove compartment. Don't put on your tie, if you wear one, until you get to work. Wear comfortable driving shoes, and switch to your work shoes when you arrive. Make sure your radio, cassette or CD player, and heater and air conditioner are in good working order. Whatever you can do to make your drive more comfortable and pleasant will be well worth the effort or expense.

If your vehicle is equipped for it, you can always use your driving time to make phone calls, touch base with clients or co-workers, and get the ball rolling even before you get to work. If you wish, you can also use one of those newfangled hand-held or voice-activated recorders during your drive to make verbal notes, record ideas, or make reminders you'll find useful. Just don't get so wrapped up in this drive-time busy-work that you find yourself wrapped around someone else's bumper.

Even if you aren't commuting to the big city, you're still likely to have work-related drive time, so plan accordingly. Whether you're running your own business away from home, travelling around the country hawking your wares, commuting to your free-lance assignment, or even picking up parts for industrial assembly work at home, you are going to depend on your car. Once you get behind the wheel, you will appreciate the time and effort you have spent making your car comfortable to drive.

Whether you're a nurse, an engineer, a publisher, a butcher, baker, or candlestick maker, moving to the country does not mean a standing appointment in the welfare line. Despite the rather discouraging current unemployment statistics, there are plenty of jobs and careers awaiting those who are diligent, enterprising, and adaptable enough to find them. You can indeed have your country home and a satisfying, rewarding way of making a living to go with it.

CHAPTER V

"I'm Telling You, Maurice, The Fatback Is Sublime..."

❖

(The joys of eating in the country)

Food: The Great Misconception

One of the great misconceptions about living in the country is that the daily menu resembles something out of *The Beverly Hillbillies*.

'Tain't so, Jed.

Would-be gourmets, finicky eaters, and those of you who can't quite picture yourself savoring the taste of baked possum, take heart. You don't have to leave your preference for fine dining behind when you move to less populated climes. You're not apt to miss very many of your favorite dishes.

True, your average, sleepy little village isn't hiding many four-star restaurants, and master chefs don't normally ply their trade in places like Antville, Ohio or Lone Jack, Missouri. But these days, most country areas boast restaurants and grocery stores with surprisingly varied food choices that can satisfy the most discriminating palates. Okay, so you might have a little trouble ordering out for Chinese, but by and large if you can sup on it in the city you can hog it down in the country.

And if you simply *insist* on more exotic fare—and the prices that go with it—all you have to do is drive a little. Most rural families today don't live that far from places offering everything from tofu to a tongue sandwich. Country people like to chow down on some fancy grub once in a while, too, you know. And you can still make it home in plenty of time to watch *Nightline*.

You may also have to travel a bit to grab a Big Mac or visit the Colonel. But fast-food joints dot the landscape with monotonous regularity, and french fries, a Coke, and a Mc-You-Name-It are rarely far from anyone's door.

As for those local, not-so-fast food restaurants, what they may lack in atmosphere—whatever that is—they make up in full, satisfying meals, friendly service, and common-sense prices. And, it's not all just stick-to-your-ribs, good old meat-and-potatoes, come-and-get-it-Andy-and-Opie cuisine, either. News of the perils of cholesterol and the joys of a fine, well-prepared salad reached the ears of even the most countrified country-restaurant owners a long time ago. Plus you'll never have to endure sulky, surly waiters or overpriced, underdone meals again. What more could you ask from a restaurant?

There's a special bonus for all you carnivores out there: In the country, everything from pork chops to mutton to filet mignon can be had fresh from a local slaughterhouse. (That might be a little *too* fresh for some of the more squeamish, but if you're a meat-eater it really doesn't get any better than that.) It's also hard to beat the taste of chicken right off the farm or fish fresh-caught from local lakes and streams.

Let 'em try eating fresh-caught fish in Manhattan.

Eatin' In

When it comes to dining at home (where you probably eat most of your meals anyway), you can make grocery runs in the country that would have Julia Child and the Galloping Gourmet fighting to ride in your trunk. Besides the grocery stores with their surprisingly varied food choices, there are also roadside stands a'plenty offering really fresh fruits and vegetables. Whatever grows in your rural region, and some things that don't, can be found at these little "fresh food marts" located along country roads everywhere. Also, neighboring farmers often offer their extra produce for sale. Front-yard signs such as "Eggs By The Dozen," "Honey For Sale," and "Sweet Corn Sold Here" are as common as Elvis sightings in Memphis.

And then there are the bake sales.

Mouth-watering, lip-smacking—whatever the adjectives of your choice—bake sales. Just picture long tables heavy-laden with delicious pies, cakes, cookies, and other culinary treats. Homemade goodies, actually made at home, and trundled to storefronts, fire halls, and community centers to be offered up, at more-than-reasonable prices, for your conspicuous consumption.

Often a means of fund-raising for various organizations or charities, bake sales let country residents enjoy the home-baked pleasures of chocolate chip cookies, pecan pies, brownies—the whole line-up of "forbidden" desserts—without actually having to do any home-baking. Country bake sales are held year-round. Aside from special events such as bazaars or street fairs, community participation is particularly high during the holidays, with many a Christmas candy-cane cookie or Halloween pumpkin pie being bought up and wolfed down at these celebrations of country neighborliness.

If you would like to show off your own personal baking abilities or use your secret family recipe to wow the local townsfolk, rest assured that you will be welcome to contribute the specialty of your choice to any bake sale. (This is also a good way to start getting to know your new country neighbors.) The best entrees are sturdy and portable, like fruit pies, rather than light and fragile, like chiffon pies, in order to withstand the rigors of bake sale conditions and transactions. (Alison Boteler's cookbook, *The Great American Bake Sale*, a fascinating look at these familiar but seldom-described events, offers lots of helpful advice and insight for would-be contributors and customers alike.)

Just How Does Your Garden Grow?

One of the distinct advantages of rural life is having land to do with as you wish. Even if you choose not to be a farmer, you still have the option of growing at least some of your own food. You probably won't be able to feed the multitudes or even live solely off of what you're able to raise yourself. But a decent-size backyard garden, tended with water and a little loving care, can produce a surprising amount of...well, just about anything you feel like planting that will grow in your neck of the woods. And food doesn't get any fresher or cheaper than that.

If you're new to growing edibles, keep your garden on the small side. It's better to grow a few things well than to court failure by taking on too much at once. You can always grow more the following season. Make a list of some of your favorite vegetables, find out which ones grow well in your area, and plant a modest amount. Gardens require care—the more you plant, the more time you will need to spend gardening.

In deciding where to put your garden, one of the first considerations is to find a place close to the house so you won't have to walk a long way just to get to it. But other things may be more important. The soil itself must be capable of sustaining a garden. You'll need good drainage, too—your garden doesn't belong in the middle of a low spot that turns into a big puddle every time it rains. Try to find a place with a crumbly loam soil. Unlike sandy soils or dense clay, the loam provides decent drainage while still retaining moisture for plant roots.

You'll also want to pick the sunniest spot you can find, one that provides at least five to six hours of direct sunlight a day. If you can't find a place offering both suitable soil and direct sunlight, go with the best soil, and plant vegetables that don't need all-day sun. Plants like beets, broccoli, cabbage, leaf lettuce, chives, peas, and spinach will produce a decent harvest with even less than five hours of daily sunlight.

How much watering you'll have to do will depend on your choice of plants and Mother Nature. If it's not raining enough to keep your crop happy, you'll need to spring for a Lawn Boy or a Rain Bird or else get out the watering can. Just make sure you find out how much water your plants really need. You can actually drown some plants that do well without a lot of water.

Finally, if your rural home gets a little on the windy side at times, you can build a windbreak to protect taller plants like sweet corn. Just make sure the windbreak is set far enough away that it doesn't cast a sunlight-blocking shadow on your garden.

Once you've selected your plants and decided on the general size and location of your garden, it's time to lay it out. It helps to draw the layout so you can see the relationships between the land and the plants. Most gardeners use the trusty single-row method of gardening. But if space is a consideration you may be able to "get

Vegetable Timetable

Depending on variety, here are the approximate growing periods for some of the more popular vegetables.

Beans...*60-90 days*	**Eggplant**...*70 days*
Brussel Sprouts...*90 days*	**Lettuce**...*45 days*
Cabbage...*50-100 days*	**Peas**...*60-65 days*
Cauliflower...*45-65 days*	**Spinach**...*60 days*
Celery...*110 days*	**Squash**...*50 days*
Corn...*100 days*	**Tomatoes**...*45-95 days*
Cucumber...*50-60 days*	**Watermelon**...*80 days*

more in" in a certain area by curving the bed or simply by setting your plants out in clumps instead of rows.

Include your plants in the layout so you can see how they will interact. Plants which require plenty of sun will not grow as well in the shade of taller plants. Keep plants with similar soil, light, and moisture needs in the same area of your garden. Sample the many gardening books and magazines on the market to learn about such practices as "companion planting" which maximizes the harvest, and "succession planting" which makes the most efficient use of garden space.

Like huge farm fields, your garden will benefit from crop rotation. Move the nonperennials to different spots each season. Plant a leaf crop where a root crop grew last year. If you vary what you plant and where you plant it from year to year, your garden will stay as productive as possible.

And, mulch, friend, mulch. Mulching, or spreading organic plant matter on top of the soil, helps the garden by slowing moisture evaporation and helps you by reducing the time you spend watering. Mulching also helps keep weeds—and weed-pulling—to a minimum.

Just because you like certain vegetables doesn't mean they will grow in your garden. Check out other gardens in your area to find out what grows best. Learn all you can about your prospective plants and their needs for moisture, sunlight, soil, and other conditions; determine if they will prosper in your location; and plant accordingly. By paying attention to the plants and weeds growing wild on your property, you can tell a lot about the general conditions of your land. For instance, quack grass thrives in wet, acid soil, while pepperweed prefers an alkaline base, and clover thrives in a soil low in nitrogen. You can also take the more scientific approach and have your soil analyzed by a local USDA or university or county extension office.

An old country saw has it that what people need for gardening "is a cast-iron back with a hinge in it." What with planning, planting, weeding, and watering, a garden requires time, attention, and effort, especially in the first year. You also have to protect your edibles from foraging creatures, such as rabbits and deer if you hope to keep any of your vegetables for yourself. Luckily, country wisdom embraces years and years of practical experience. To keep animals from "drowning" your plants, for example, you can soak cigar butts in a jug of water for a few weeks and then use a spray bottle to spread this evil concoction in the plants' vicinity. Or, you can keep wild animals from chowing down on your vegetables by scattering dried blood around garden borders. (The local slaughterhouse can probably help you with this if the moon isn't full.)

Before you know it, you will have a garden that offers up a bountiful harvest without requiring a lot of maintenance. The rewards are more than the considerable satisfaction and pleasurable independence you'll feel. Your garden will save you money and give you the

> ### The Dandy Dandelion
>
> No one seriously recommends that you graze on your country lawn, but the fact is that properly prepared dandelions make good eating.
>
> What's more, the dandelion is rich in Vitamin C, calcium, phosphorus, and potassium, and is one of the best green-vegetable sources for Vitamin-A. And—*take this, Popeye*—the dandelion is nutritionally equal to spinach.
>
> Dandelions should be harvested when they're young and tender in early spring. (Later in the season, dandelions become bitter and stringy.) To harvest, just get yourself a knife and a sack. Put the knife in the soil at the dandelion's base, cut the tap root, and pry out the entire rosette of leaves. Collect the plants in the sack and, when you get enough, trim away the dead leaves, wash off the dirt, and you're all set. You can steam dandelion greens and serve with butter, salt, and pepper. Or you can eat them raw, add them to a fresh salad, or cook them in a stew. Some folks also say that dandelions make good wine.

luxury of having your very own produce section literally right outside your door.

Freeze 'Em And Reap

There are three essential tools for your country garden: a hoe, a watering can, and a great big freezer.

Yep, that's right. A freezer. Freezing some of your harvest lets you enjoy your vegetables even during those months when your garden lies dormant. The trick is to know what to freeze and how to freeze it. Not all vegetables take kindly to refrigeration, and even those that do need certain preparation to retain their flavor.

If you're unsure which vegetables to freeze and which to store in a cool, dry place such as a root cellar, talk to an experienced gardener, visit a garden center, or get some books on gardening, and find out what is recommended for preserving your crop. In general, those vegetables with high water content, like cucumbers, don't do very well in the freezer, while those with low water content, like peas, take it very well.

The biggest enemy of frozen vegetables is the dreaded freezer burn, which is caused by moisture in the vegetable containers. The routine opening and closing of a freezer door causes the internal temperature to fluctuate and moisture to condense on food packages. As this moisture refreezes, it burns the frozen edibles, leaving a nasty taste in your mouth when you thaw and eat them. Or *try* to eat them. Sophisticated commercial operators use flash freezing—sort of an instant arctic effect—and vacuum packing to prevent condensation inside the package, but don't worry if you don't happen to have a commercial freezing system or a vacuum packing set-up in your house. There are several things you can do to imitate the big operators and ensure yourself of unburned, good-tasting vegetables.

First, almost all vegetables should be blanched before they are frozen. For you first-time blanchers, blanching means boiling your veggies briefly in water and then dunking them in ice water. This greatly slows the aging of vegetable enzymes and helps retain freshness, taste, and vitamin potency.

Seal your vegetables in moisture-proof packaging (like plastic bags with airtight seals), in heavy-duty aluminum foil, or in rigid containers with tightly closing lids. Wax paper, old bread wrappers, and grocery-store produce bags are strictly short-term, since this type of packaging is far from airtight. Allow for expansion by leaving a little air space (but no air) in rigid containers. Filling them to within an inch of the rim is about right for keeping out excess air. If you use flexible packaging, press as much air out as possible before sealing.

Freeze your vegetables as quickly as possible to minimize condensation. Be sure your containers are cool before you place them in the freezer. Since small packages freeze more quickly than large ones, package accordingly. Crank the freezer temperature down as cold as it will go. If possible, leave a little space around each package to speed up the freezing process.

If you keep the freezer temperature no higher than zero degrees Fahrenheit, your vegetables should retain their taste for a good ten months. Just as vegetables benefit from quick initial freezing, they should be thawed quickly as well for the best flavor. Have boiling water ready, chuck in the frozen edibles, and get ready to dig in. (If your vegetables have been thawed for more than twenty-four hours, don't try to refreeze them, unless you are trying to kill the flavor as a way of preventing the in-laws from inviting themselves over for dinner again.)

Tree For Yourself

Besides gardening, another way to grow your own is to plant fruit trees or, better yet, to take advantage of the trees already growing on your land. Depending on where you live, you can enjoy ample harvests of apples, cherries, oranges, and so many other delectable fruits, many varieties of which are never found in urban or suburban grocery stores. Most fruits explode with flavor when eaten right off the tree. You can use your fruit harvest to bake apple dumplings or cherry pies or to make some of the best fruit juice you have ever tasted. If you grow apples, you can let the juice age until it gets to be good old hard cider, which will leave you with a good old hangover if you drink enough of it.

Trees produce more than fruit. Chestnuts, for one tasty example. Longfellow was probably eating off the same spreading chestnut tree he was writing about. Chestnuts can be used in a variety of mouth-watering ways. You can mash them as a substitute for potatoes, use them in stuffing or, yes, Virginia, keep them "roasting on an open fire" for a sweet-tasting snack. (Some say that chestnuts roast a whole lot easier, and wind up a whole lot tastier, if you boil them in water for five minutes or so before you roast them.)

Like fruit trees, it's a lot more convenient if you already have mature chestnut trees on your property supplying you with their natural harvest. But chestnut trees grow quickly enough for you to expect a decent chestnut supply within four or five years of planting.

If you are fortunate enough to have maple trees on your land, consider yourself truly blessed. It takes a bit of doing to collect the sap and boil it down, but there are few country dishes that taste better than a big stack of hot-off-the-griddle pancakes smothered in fresh maple syrup. Unless it's hot-from-the-iron waffles smothered in fresh maple syrup. Or, for that matter, *anything* smothered in fresh maple syrup. Real syrup is country-good eatin' and not that hard to collect if you know how to go about it.

Early spring is the time for sap-collecting, and the "sugaring season," as it's called, runs about six weeks. You'll only need a few tools to tap your trees: a brace-and-bit, a sap spout, a hammer, and a bucket with a handle and lid. Make sure your tree is at least ten inches in diameter, then drill a hole about chest-high in the trunk. Use the hammer to tap in your sap spout, then hang the bucket on it to collect the sap. The bucket lid will keep out rain and dirt. Trees greater than fifteen inches in diameter can take more than one tap. A country rule-of-thumb says that trees from ten to fifteen inches should get one tap; trees from fifteen to twenty inches, two taps; twenty to twenty-five inches, three taps; and greater than twenty-five inches, four. Check your taps daily to make sure the buckets aren't overflowing. How fast the sap runs will depend on the weather. It might run steadily for a day or two, then quit for a week. However fast you collect it, don't let the sap sit too long before boiling it into syrup. Sap takes only a day or two to ferment under normal conditions, and fermented sap produces dark and bad-tasting syrup. Even if the weather is cold, you can safely store the sap for only two or three days before boiling.

If you're a real do-it-yourselfer, you can boil the sap down into syrup yourself. This can involve a lot of time, effort, and expense, however. You may need to build a sugar house to boil the sap in and lay in equipment such as a wood-fire evaporator and storage tanks. Happily, wherever you find maple trees, you'll also find outfits that earn an occasional dollar by boiling other peoples' sap into syrup. Most folks are glad to give them the business.

Meats That Ain't Red

Red meat has come in for quite a bit of adverse publicity as a source of cholesterol and saturated fat. But not all meat is red, and no one in the country is going to shun you if you don't care for the taste of steak. The country, in fact, has a number of very acceptable, healthy alternatives to red meat.

If you're the fishing type, you'll delight in using local fishin' holes to help add variety to your table. Trout, bass, bluegill—whatever the local fare. Just reel 'em in (provided they're biting), bring 'em home, and savor the taste of *fresh* fish. And like vegetables, fresh fish can be frozen for the months when the pond is frozen over.

Raising chickens, another popular source of fresh meat in the country, offers the additional bonus of regular omelets. A good laying hen will lay a little more than one egg every two days, so a flock of twelve to twenty chickens will supply the needs of most couples and their children. (You won't need a rooster if all you want are the eggs.) Hens, which start laying at about five to six months of age, will normally live about twelve years if they don't run afoul of a weasel, some other chicken thief, or your own frying pan.

Once your coop is built and your birds are settled in, all you have to do is add a little chicken feed on a regular basis, and you're in business.

For those chickens making the cut, so to speak, for Sunday dinner, younger birds are likely to be healthier and tastier than their elders. The old method of lopping off their heads with an axe is passé (but still darn effective), since anything less than a good clean cut can be a little rough on the chicken. Besides, some of today's citizens are sensitive to the sight of a headless chicken galloping around the yard. Nowadays, the proper procedure is to immobilize the chicken in a device known as a killing cone and to use a thin, sharp blade called—what else?—a killing knife to stab the chicken through the brain. It's not as gruesome as it sounds. The chicken never knows what hit her, and, curiously, the modern method somehow causes chicken feathers to loosen, making plucking that much easier. (This is relative. You'll probably still have to boil the carcass to make plucking convenient. Incidentally, don't let anyone tell you to do this indoors. Few things in the world stink as badly as boiling chicken carcasses and feathers.)

As for pork, that "other white meat," raising pigs and hogs—a hog is a pig that weighs at least 120 pounds—is a little different from catching a fish or raising a few chickens. It's a lot different, actually. Most of us know, at least roughly, how to go about catching fish, and the majority of people can learn to raise chickens and gather eggs without too much difficulty. But raising livestock, as the bigger animals like cows, sheep, goats, and swine are called, is not for the novice. Livestock are more complicated and more trouble to take care of, requiring more know-how and experience to raise successfully. Besides, animal husbandry is a lot more costly than buying a fishing pole or a little chicken feed. Unless you are confident that you know what you're doing or are willing to take the time to learn, livestock raising is best left to professional farmers.

Whether you dabble in chickens or dedicate your life to livestock, there is one last, vital piece of advice: don't name any of your animals. It's one things to send some nameless beef cow off to the slaughterhouse, but looking Brownie in the eye and telling her that her days are numbered is enough to choke up a used car salesman. And if your kids happen to discover that it is Buttercup or SugarPlum on your kitchen table, they might begin to regard you as the local arch-fiend. What's more, you're likely to feel as if you deserve it.

Wetting Your Whistle

If you have a yen for John Barleycorn and a place to guzzle it in, the country offers plenty of shot-and-a-beer bars, featuring a variety of star and wannabe-star barmaids and bartenders and lots of Hank Williams Jr. and Randy Travis on the jukebox. If you prefer drinking alone, or with someone in private, you can get your booze to go. And there's always that hard cider.

If you like a Lowenbrau with your power lunch, there are more than a few better-class lounges around, along with their resident collections of lounge lizards and lizardettes. To say nothing of live bands rocking, if not around the clock, at least until the wee hours of the morning, and big-screen TVs showing big-time sports, movies, Nielson favorites, and everything else.

Country establishments have even been known to serve an occasional Perrier. You can even find a good Bordeaux in most areas, if you know where to look and don't mind paying less than you may be used to.

As for more plebeian drink choices, Coke, Kool-Aid, and iced tea are Coke, Kool-Aid, and iced tea, whether you're in Paris or Podunk.

Water is a different matter. There's isn't a city anywhere that has anything to match the overall purity and taste of the good old country water that comes from the good old country wells where so many good old country homes get their water.

Wells are relatively simple to maintain. Most are mechanical to some degree, so there may be occasional problems. But most wells operate flawlessly for years. Regular, routine check-ups by local professionals will usually insure early detection and correction of any potential problems.

Another advantage of water in the country is its low cost. If you own the property, you own the well and the water. There's no water bill to pay, this month or any month. All you have to pay for is the electricity to run the pump and maybe a hand pump for when lightning hits the power line. Even if you have to have your well dug—don't do it by yourself—country water is still a real bargain.

Unfortunately, modern life has not always been kind to the water supply. There is a certain risk of contamination to home wells from legal and illegal industrial chemicals, landfill seepage, agricultural pesticides, and increased oil and gas drilling. Fortunately, Love Canal is the exception. The Environmental Protection Agency reports that less than two per cent of American ground water has been contaminated and that much of this has occurred around industrial centers located far from most country wells. And even most agricultural pesticides have to be highly concentrated and applied nearby in large amounts before they pose significant health dangers.

Nevertheless, contamination is not a trivial concern. If you suspect your rural well has become, or is in danger of becoming, contaminated from any source, a professional well contractor or the nearest health department can test your water. If you haven't yet purchased the property and you suspect that contaminants might be a problem, insist on a water test before you come to terms with the owner.

Fortunately, country water sources are overwhelmingly safe, providing good, clean, tasty drinking water for millions of rural inhabitants. All with no "mediciney" city-water taste, since there's no chlorine added. Or needed, thank you.

No wonder that darn Jethro looked so healthy.

CHAPTER VI

That's Entertainment

❖

(Things to do in the country)

Same Things, Only Different

People who have never lived in the country have been overheard saying that "there's nothing to do out there" for entertainment, sophisticated leisure activities, or having fun, except perhaps for an occasional quilting bee or taffy pull.

Don't bet the farm on it, friend.

Just about anything that George Cityslicker does in his metropolitan spare time can be enjoyed by Luke Hayseed in the country. Indeed, Luke probably can choose from more entertainment opportunities than George, considering that he has the Great Outdoors to work with in addition to the many indoor activities within his reach.

That's not to say that the experience is the same. Some differences may indeed exist between leisure activities in the city and those in the country—even if they happen to be the very same leisure activities.

> ## Why The Country *Needs* TV
>
> Current-events and entertainment programming from other regions, along with the national news shows, documentaries, and other current-issues programs available on Cable, have exposed people in the country to ideas and points of view that they may not have considered or even heard much about BC (Before Cable). This entertainment and cultural diversity actually combats rural isolationism and closed-mindedness. City folks may suffer from so much outside stimuli that they rightly look to the country as a place of escape. Country folk need to guard against the opposite extreme, the possibility that they will become isolated from the outside stimuli that inspire open-mindedness and breed ingenuity and inventiveness. As peculiar as it may sound, country people actually *need* to watch TV in order to keep their horizons broad and to gain exposure to other ways of life and thinking. It may be hard to regard a medium that brings us *Jake and the Fatman* as a cultural necessity, but the power of TV—and especially cable-TV—to inform, educate, and inspire is one reason for the general sophistication of today's country.

Take TV, for instance. Watching the boob-tube is a pretty common practice no matter where you live. In a recent Life Style Study performed by ad agency giant, DDB Needham Worldwide, fifty-three per cent of Americans named TV-viewing as their primary form of entertainment. But there is a crucial difference between watching TV in the city and watching it in the country, a difference that can be traced to cable-TV.

Cable had its beginnings sometime in the 1950s, somewhere in the hills of Pennsylvania where ordinary TV reception ranges between impossible and merely unviewable. It took a while to catch on, but during the last decade or so cable systems and satellite dishes have spread through virtually all areas of the nation, city and country alike.

No longer is TV confined to local stations or "Big 3" network programming. Much cable-TV is now local TV gone national. Country viewers can now get a feel for how other people in other places live, work, and play. You can sit in the comfort of a West Virginia living room and let WGN fill you in on what Chicagoans think about the latest political scandal, or you can switch on a set in Vermont and find out what's new in Atlanta. Cable has helped cosmopolitanize the country by allowing even the most rural families to stay up-to-date on everything that's going on, everywhere in the world, in a way that network TV never did. Cable also brings to the country thought-provoking, sophisticated forms of entertainment and education that were once available only in urbanized areas. Even if you live in the middle of the Mojave Desert, you can still get to see Josephine Baker do the Banana Dance.

Well, not entirely. Some parts of the country, believe it or not, still have no cable systems, so you might have to adorn your property with a satellite dish if you want to get all the programs that you watched in the city. You might think about doing this even if there is a cable system in your new rural community. Some of the smaller country cable outfits don't offer all that many channels or all that much in the way of cultural exposure. You may *need* to go with a dish to get the programs and diversity that you would like. True, they're not very pretty, but at least in the country you are more likely to have a place to put your dish and less likely to find that a sky-scraper is cutting off your reception.

So you and your big-screen move to the boondocks, tune in CNN, and climb aboard the couch-potato truck, right? No, no, no. As important as television can be, it is hardly the only source of culture or entertainment in

> ### Satellite Dishes
>
> It used to be that if you wanted to pull in the better satellite stations for your home-viewing, you had to have a satellite dish about the size of a '65 Buick on top of your house.
> Not anymore. Small dish antennas, some measuring no more than four feet, are starting to hit the mass market.
> These unobtrusively smaller dishes range from around $750 for the basic unit to some $2000 for the top-of-the-line model.
> Important features to consider when purchasing your dish include the positioner, which moves the antenna from one satellite to another; the descrambler, which enables reception of some or all of the approximately 70 pay channels available; and the receiver, which determines the power bands and stations the dish will actually be able to deliver to your tv set.

the country. Remember, most of the things you can do in the city you can also do in rural areas. If movie-going is one of your favorite activities, as it is for so many people, you'll be glad to know that moving to the country will not deprive you of the latest from Hollywood. You may have to drive a bit to get to the nearest *MovieWorld*, but, given the facts of country travel, the well-known "theater near you" probably *is* relatively nearby.

Living in the country also allows you to enjoy a movie-watching institution that is slowly, sadly, disappearing from the landscape: the drive-in. There's nothing quite like the scratchy-speaker, horn-honking, raunchy-hot-dog-and-stale-popcorn experience of watching your favorite flicks (that's *flicks*, in plural—drive-ins traditionally offer two-for-the-price-of-one double features) at the local drive-in. Plus, you don't have to put up with the crumbling of candy-paper, the crunching of popcorn, or the whispering of conversation by the jerk sitting behind you, unless he came with you.

Don't care to venture out to watch movies? Okay. You can always take advantage of the local video store. Country video rental places are as common as VCRs themselves. Moreover, many rural convenient marts and grocery stores have gotten in on the act—and the profits—of renting videotapes to the viewing public. Finding movies to pop into your VCR is seldom a problem, no matter where you call home.

Of course there is more to life than TV and movies. Concerts, art museums, plays, personal appearances, dinner theater—they're all just a routine drive away for most folks. Even comedy clubs are becoming more and more common in the boondock everywhere. Before you decide that it all sounds like too much time spent in the car, consider how much time you spend driving to entertainment in the city, waiting in lines, looking for parking places, etc. Chances are that travel times aren't going to be that much different anywhere. And in the country, travel is part of the entertainment, not an adventure in itself.

Shopping is another "city pastime" which you can fully enjoy in the country. So what if you have to drive a little to cruise the nearest mall or shopping center? Once you're there you can buy all the same new fashions you would have bought in the city or try on any of the latest creations from Frederick's of Hollywood. There are always local stores, too. Anything you have the money for usually can be found somewhere close by. And if it can't, you will quickly learn why country residents have come to appreciate mail order. Mail order houses, department stores, and the Home Shopping Network are just three of the many distributors which have discovered the large profits waiting to be made from catering to country consumers. All you need is a telephone and a credit card or a checkbook, and you can have whatever-it-is delivered right to your doorstep.

If you like to browse flea markets, search out antiques, or attend auctions, you're going to love the country. Flea markets are found everywhere, especially during warm-weather months. The discriminating shopper can pick up great bargains on everything from electric tools to books to handmade furniture. Many antique shops can also be found in rural parts, with prices for authentic antiques typically far more reasonable than those charged by urban antique dealers for borderline ones. Private estate sales, auction barns, and auction houses are open year 'round. Larger items, such as cars and boats, are usually sold in auction barns, which seldom offer much in the way of chairs or heating. Auction houses, usually with chairs and heat, are generally where you'll find household items such as toasters and tables or jewelry and junk. Estate sales are almost always held in private houses. Here, too, you can count on prices substantially below what you would pay at retail or even in a normal secondhand store. And there's always the possibility of discovering that occasional rare treasure to enhance your collection—or your bank account.

The joys of reading are magnified in the country. Because of the generally quieter environment and easier pace of life, it is perhaps easier to relax and read in the country than anywhere else. Reading is a popular form of diversion for many country folk, and there's no shortage of country libraries and book stores which offer both new and secondhand editions. And even in the remotest rural areas, mail order puts book clubs and bookstores as close as your mailbox.

Sports lovers don't have to live in Chicago to root for the Bulls, Bears, White Sox, Cubs, or Black Hawks. You can attend most of their games via cable or satellite. And there's more to the sporting life than professional teams. You will be more than pleasantly surprised at the number of semi-professional and college teams play-

Music To Your Ears

You don't *have* to become a country-western music fan when you move to the country. Your classical music CDs will play just as clearly in the boonies, your jazz recordings will have the same resonances as when you lived in the city, and your rural radio will bring everything from rock'n'roll to opera.

Still, you can figure on being exposed to C&W a bit more often in the country. There will probably be more country selections on the jukebox, a larger CW section in the record stores, and a few more local radio stations devoted to "the golden sounds of country."

After you listen a while, country music begins to grow on you. Even if you don't consider yourself the country music type, you may begin seeking out the croonings of Randy Travis or Charley Pride, the rollicking rowdiness of Hank Williams, Jr., or the soulful beltings of Dolly Parton or Loretta Lynn. Before you know it, you might even be passing up the sitcoms or the Larry King show in favor of Ralph Emery and *Nashville Now*.

Even if you never stop preferring The Four Tops or Fleetwood Mac, it's hard to imagine that anyone who appreciates good music wouldn't enjoy at least some country music. If nothing else, you can understand the lyrics without being outraged. You might not be ready to trade in the Metropolitan Opera for the Grand Old Opry, but don't be surprised if you find yourself tapping your foot just a little.

---

ing every imaginable sport on country fields and in country arenas. Many towns sponsor or provide facilities for sports leagues of all types. Anyone with an interest can usually get on a team for such sports as men and women's softball, volleyball, basketball, flag football, and more. There are also golf teams, and countless countryside golf courses where you don't have any trouble getting a decent tee-off time or spend most of your links time waiting for the foursome in front to let you play through.

A Hiking You Can Go

Another activity easily and conveniently enjoyed in the country is walking in all of its forms. Hiking, walking, and jogging are excellent forms of exercise enjoyed by health-conscious individuals everywhere who regularly hike, walk, and jog their ways to lower blood pressure and improved physical well-being. But country walkers have an important advantage over city walkers. They don't have to join a gym, drive to the nearest jogging path, or invest in a home treadmill to take advantage of the salutary and aesthetic benefits of hiking, jogging, and similar activities.

The country offers plenty of the wide open spaces and hilly terrain that you need for walking activities. All you need to get are the appropriate shoes. Walking or jogging along country roads, with their scarcity of traffic and abundance of clean air and picturesque scenery, is a truly enjoyable way of keeping yourself in shape. Paved or unpaved, the country is a delightful place to meander around in and explore, away from the hustle and bustle of city life and the artificiality of city parks, mall walks, and hiking tours.

If your rural part of the country is blessed with the right weather, there's another form of walking that you can look forward to: cross-country skiing. You'll need to get skis and some other gear, but it's worth the investment. The advantages are the same as with walking or jogging—aerobic benefits and scenic enjoyment without the need to join a club or invest in a NordicTrack. And every country path or pasture turns into new and challenging terrain with every fresh snowfall. You don't need acres of land on which to build your own ski trail, though some fanatics have done even that. Just seek out a nearby logging road, rail bed, or tractor lane, wait for a good snow day, and discover a glorious side of nature that the city forgot a long time ago.

The country virtually invites you to hike, walk, or run to your heart's content without forcing you to rub elbows with too many people or navigate through man-made distractions. Opportunities for pleasurable exercise are close, convenient, healthy, and free. So, get hiking already. You'll enjoy it.

You Don't Have To Be Named 'Bubba'

Camping. Hunting. Fishing. These are recreations that can be found only in the country. Admittedly, they're not for everybody. But for some they offer pure pleasure. And you don't need to wear coveralls, chew tobacco, or drive a pick-up truck with a gun rack in order to share in these and other recreational opportunities available in the Great Country Outdoors.

All you need for camping out, for instance, is a few pieces of equipment and an appropriate location. At the minimum, camping requires a tent or at least a sleeping bag, waterproof matches, a compass, and a supply of food adequate for the time you plan on staying. (You may need water as well, unless it's available close to your campsite.) Include some warm clothes in case of cold or wet weather, especially a change or two of wool socks and some gloves. A first-aid kit is a wise precaution, particularly if you plan on staying awhile. Take along a roll or two of tissue paper, or even some paper towels. It will save you from some unpleasant experiments with pine cones.

There are only a few rules of thumb for choosing a campsite. Don't camp under tall trees that may attract lightning or drop a wind-blown limb on your head.

(Country folk often refer to such trees as "widow-makers.") Avoid dry grass or heavy brush around the campsite—nothing is more out of control than an out-of-control brush fire. And don't settle near swamps or marshy ground, unless you think mosquito swatting is good exercise.

Hunting, with either gun or bow, is a popular country sport. Hunters are often misunderstood and maligned. They are rarely cold-hearted, bloodthirsty killers with red necks and missing molars. Most are just as concerned about the survival of animal species as anyone else—after all, no animals, no hunting—but they also realize that saving wildlife is as much a matter of preserving natural habitat as preventing overhunting.

If you do choose to hunt, certain parts of the American countryside are natural meccas for hunters. The usual quarry is deer, along with rabbits, ducks, and other small game. But larger animals, including even bears and moose, can be hunted in some regions.

Most firearm hunting is done with long-barrelled weapons. Rifles are designed to shoot bullets with reasonable accuracy up to two or three hundred yards, while shotguns shoot hundreds of tiny pellets in an expanding pattern, with a maximum effective range of no more than fifty yards. (Some folks do hunt with handguns, but you have to be pretty experienced to be successful at it.) Make sure the gun you use is the right one for your intended game. A firearm appropriate for big game would probably be too big for smaller animals, while a gun suitable for small game wouldn't bring down bigger targets.

Whatever you're hunting, there will be a proper season for it and probably a limit on the number you can take. You'll also need a current hunting license unless you want to risk the wrath of local rangers. It shouldn't need to be said, but treat every gun as if it were loaded. Make sure the bore is kept clear at all times, and if you do drop your gun in the snow or mud, check it immediately for obstructions. Take care when shooting toward hard, flat surfaces or toward water, both of which may cause ricochets.

The secret to bow-hunting is practice, and lots of it. Fifty yards is a long shot for most bow hunters. Since you don't usually get a second shot when hunting, you'll need to learn how to get in close and make every arrow count. An experienced archer can help you refine your technique. Hay or straw bales make excellent target backstops for practicing and will help you learn your personal range for the day when you go on the actual hunt.

Not all local laws require you to wear the bright orange vest or hat common to hunters. *Wear them anyway.* Hunting can be great fun, but it can also be dangerous. Every year too many people are victims of fatal and unnecessary hunting accidents. So always take more care than you have to, even if you know that you're just an innocent bystander and that nothing is going to happen to you.

You don't have to hunt in order to enjoy shooting guns or bows. You can always target shoot at the many country gun clubs which maintain safe facilities and even hold regular shooting contests. Archery ranges are less common, but it's easy enough to set up practice targets of your own in a location which is secluded enough to avoid endangering anyone else.

Many who don't hunt or even target practice with guns or with bows shoot local game with another instrument: the camera. Taking pictures of country flora and fauna is a wonderful way to enjoy the wildlife and the countryside. With a little practice you'll be capturing beautiful, natural scenes and action shots that you'll want to keep forever. And the countryside is a great place for bird watchers to seek out cedar waxwings, prothonotary warblers, yellow-crowned night herons, or any other of the winged wonders which frequent the open countryside.

Fishing is a lot less controversial. Unlike hunting, fishing seems almost a pacifist's pastime, conjuring up boyish dreams of playing hooky and the ol' fishin' hole. It's not a coincidence that the classic image of a business executive off pursuing his own interests for the day is an empty desk and a simple, hand-lettered sign that reads, *Gone Fishin'*. Fishing is a lot safer than hunting, too. You might fall out of the boat or get a hook in your finger, but the only real danger most country fishermen face is falling asleep and missing supper.

Most parts of the country boast a local fishing spot—a lake, a river or a stream, a crick or a pond. Some places boast lots of them. You can use everything from a dropline to a plain bamboo pole to a fiberglass rod and reel to fish with and everything from nightcrawlers to grasshoppers to minnows for bait. If you are fishing for something specific, it will help to know something about lures like spinners and spoons. A local fisherman or someone at the nearest bait and tackle shop can fill you in on what's best to use, and why, in your local fishing hole.

You can fish from a boat. You can fish from a pier or off the side of a bridge. Or from right off the land, standing up or sitting under a tree if you're close enough to the water. Or you can wade out a little, if you've got the boots for it.

If you have a boat to fish from, you can even pass up the fishing in favor of boating or water-skiing, two more of the abundant recreational opportunities found in the country. Or, you can go canoeing or kayaking. Or you might just go swimming, for which you don't need a boat at all. (You can go swimming in the city or suburbs too, if you can find a pool that isn't too crowded. Somehow, though, it just isn't the same as having an entire pond or lake to splash around in.)

During cold months, you probably won't be doing much swimming or camping out. But you can still hunt, and you might try your hand at ice-fishing. Ice-fishing involves the standard fishing tackle, plus something to knock or drill a hole in the ice with, and lots and lots of warm clothing. You'll also need to make very sure that the ice is thick enough to hold you.

When it snows, you can also go snowmobiling. Jetting around the countryside on these "winter motorcycles" can be great fun as long as you are familiar with the terrain before you take off for parts unknown. Snow can hide dangerous ruts and camouflage fences, so it helps to know the land before you set out. You don't want to learn the hard way where the barbed wire is.

There are many outdoor sports and activities to experience in the country, so many that it would be impossible to name and describe them all. Even if you don't think of yourself as the outdoors type, you may find that living in the country lures you into discovering the Great Outdoors in ways you never dreamed you would.

Community Organizations and Local Events

The country has its share of community events and regularly-held, special forms of entertainments. There are county fairs, with everything from harness races to Demolition Derbys, mule and tractor pulls to rodeos to midway rides and amusements. Local racetracks provide facilities for race horses and trotters and stock cars. There are YMCAs, and YWCAs, if not right in town then within driving distance; aerobics classes and karate classes and sign language classes; classes for self-help and just about anything you might take an interest in. For more formal instruction, there are community colleges or state universities just like those in metropolitan areas but a whole lot less crowded. There are periodic car shows and carnivals; local Homecoming Days with chicken barbecues and bingo and bean-bag tosses and pie-eating contests; Little League baseball and high-school sports contests of all kinds; men's club events, women's club events, professional wrestling shows, local theater efforts, miniature golf courses, and so much more. You can find bar room bands everywhere, and even male and female strip shows and other bawdy entertainment, if that is your taste.

Another popular and enjoyable way of spending free time in the country is to join one or more community organizations. Even the smallest towns often contain card clubs and civic leagues, volunteer fire departments, historical societies, conservation associations, and other voluntary groups. Such organizations can always use more people, foot soldiers and generals alike. And if there isn't a local group involved in an activity you're interested in, you can always start your own. You might begin a community theater, head up a local Boy or Girl Scouts troop, form a reading tutor group. Country people are often on the lookout for new and different diversions, so it's usually not that hard to drum up a little interest in whatever it is that interests you.

"Nothing to do in the country," they say?

CHAPTER VII

Won't You Be My Neighbor?

❖

(People, life, and living in the country.)

Who's There?

People who live in the country are as diverse a group of people as you'll meet anywhere. True, there aren't as many people in rural areas—that's one of the attactions—but no matter how small and quiet the country town, you can't avoid running into at least a few people every day. Who are these people? They're everybody. All ages, all sizes, all heights, all weights. Democrats, Republicans, and Independents. The dignified, the undignified, the certified wacko. The shrewd and the not-so-shrewd, the short and the tall, the egghead and the hayseed...you get the picture. You'll find all types of people and all combinations thereof. Because country populations aren't as concentrated as urban, you probably won't see every one of these types in any given area. But if your image of the country is a place where everyone looks and acts like they belong in a Normal Rockwell painting, you're in for a surprise.

The fact is, you can't generalize about the people who live in the country any more than you can generalize about the people who live in big cities. The sort of people you'll meet in the country is going to depend on the part of the country you move to and the town you settle in. It is only natural to want to know something about the people who will be your neighbors—about their beliefs, about the ways they act and react, and, maybe most importantly, about how they're going to respond to you. It makes more than a little sense to find out something about what the people are like before you decide to make them your neighbors.

So How Do You Do That?

The best and simplest way to find out about the people in a given country place is to go and see them yourself. Even though you can't get a fix on individual residents without getting to know them personally, you can still size up a rural town and the people who live there before you actually decide to move. After all, small towns are nothing more than small groups of people who interact on a daily basis. So spend some time in the town. Walk around. Talk to the people you meet. Don't interrogate or pry, just talk. Be pleasant, respectful, and polite, and you'll find out a lot about your prosective new neighbors.

It's really not difficult to get a feel for a rural place and its inhabitants. You may find that the people of one small town seem more friendly than another. Another town might have more of an intellectual bent than some of its neighboring communities. A third town might have a greater percentage of older residents. In a sense, each small town is something of a self-contained unit with a personality shaped by the collective personalities of the people who live there. No matter what you may discover about the people of a particular country town from outside sources, nothing beats a first-hand look. You just can't tell anything for sure about people or how you'll fit in with them until you've been around them for a while.

A Scholarly Look At Country People

A number of academic studies have looked at country residents and offered some overall definitions or pictures of people who live in the country. Admittedly, no analysis, however scholarly, is going to successfully categorize all country folk or, for that matter, necessarily bear any resemblance to the people you will meet in your new rural neighborhood. Nevertheless, a number of these studies contain a good deal of insight.

One of the most interesting of these investigations was conducted in 1980 by two rural sociologists from the University of Missouri, John Holik and Herbert Lionberger. Their analysis attempted to identify the different types of country residents and to find out just why those residents stayed in the country. From their survey, Holik and Lionberger were able to divide country folk into six general categories based on their habits and beliefs.

Committed Farmers, as you might suspect, cite a commitment to farming, both as an occupation and a way of life, as their primary reason for living in the country. They regard farmers like themselves as "the backbone of the nation." They proudly embrace an altruistic country morality, believing that people in the country are more willing to lend a helping hand than their urban counterparts and that living in the country offers a community and a mutual concern rarely found elsewhere. For these and other reasons, they think the country is a superior place to raise children and that farming, by "keeping the family together," gives kids a stable basis on which to build their lives.

Reluctant Residents are generally ex-urbanites who live in the country only because they need to be close to their jobs or because they haven't found a way to move out yet. Believing that the country is too isolated from "what's going on" in the world, they may also have a hard time developing close relations with other country residents. They don't find country people to be particularly friendly or helpful. They're often ambivalent, however. While they complain that they "miss the good life" of the city, they also cite the country's scenic beauty and generally relaxed pace as important sources of emotional well-being, and they believe that living "away from nature" would be a distinct loss.

This gives them something in common with *Nature Lovers*, who give top priority to "living in harmony with nature." Attracted by the country's fresh air, peace, and natural wonders, Nature Lovers believe that the best way for people to develop truly human qualities is to live in communion with nature, where they can learn how God really meant things to be. They believe that no child should grow up without just such communion, and they live in the country in order to escape the hassles and "closed-in feelings" of life in the cities. Nature Lovers value the "humaneness" of country people, sharing the belief that rural dwellers are friendly and willing to do things for each other.

Guest of the Country live in rural areas but feel more like guests than like true country folk. They appreciate the country life style, the fresh air, the wide-open spaces, and the reprieve from the city. While they live on farms so they can "putter around" if they want, any farming they do is primarily for leisure, not profit. Regarding land ownership as a "right" that gives people independence, Guests of the Country expect such ownership to provide them with security at the end of their working careers. They find country living relaxing and worthwhile, because it always offers them something to do. They like living among farmers, whom they, too, perceive as more willing to do things for each other than city people. Like Nature Lovers, they value the country as a place to get away from the hectic pace of city life.

Child Raisers live in the country because they want to bring their up children in a clean environment where the family can spend time together. In their eyes, children brought up in rural areas can enjoy freedom while learning responsibility and respect for their elders. To Child Raisers, life in communities which are small enough for people really to know each other encourages people to be kind, helpful, and interested in other individuals as people and truly caring for children. They consider it obvious that children are happier growing up in the country. Like Nature Lovers and Guest of the Country, Child Raisers value the tranquility and fresh air of the rural environment. They appreciate the personal benefits of land ownership, such as the feelings of personal independence that owning land fosters. If they farm, it is strictly as a hobby.

Agrarian Cornerstones are attracted by the spiritual aspects of country life. They regard rural living as the natural, God-intended way of life, where people are free to worship as they please and where man-made and man-inspired interference can be kept to a minimum. They value the virtues of hard work and consider the cultivation of the land as the original destiny of mankind, whether they themselves farm or not. Agrarian Cornerstones believe that children learn far more about life from raising an animal in the country than from attending school in the city, though they do not necessarily believe that country life protects children from big city temptations. They, too, consider country dwellers to be friendly, self-reliant, and willing to help each other.

Like most generalizations, these Holik-Lionberger types are simple caricatures. You probably won't find very many people who fit cleanly into any single category. But also like most generalizations, these oversimplifications contain some truth. The ideas, hopes, and values expressed by the rural inhabitants of the study can be found among individuals and groups throughout the countryside. If you find yourself in sympathy with even some of these feelings, you may well discover a community of like-minded neighbors in your new country home.

Country Kids, Country Life

If you have kids, your move to the country will have to take them into consideration. Certainly, you'll want answers to questions such as: What are children like in the country? Are they really all like Opie? How are they different from urban youth? What will life be like there for my kids? What about schools? What about day care?

In case you need reassurance...no, kids in the country are not all like Opie. Kids are basically kids, no matter where they live, and young people in the country resemble young urbanites far more than they differ from them. More than anything, what distinguishes kids in the country from kids in the city is the environment. Not just the natural surroundings, but the small-town atmosphere, including the small schools with small enrollments.

You don't have to be a Nature Lover or a Child Raiser to appreciate the natural advantages of growing up in the country. Fresh air, green grass, babbling brooks, cows grazing on the hillside, children with all outdoors to play in—it's all pretty idyllic. It's all true, too. The country *is* a beautiful, wonderful place to be a kid, a place of communion with nature, a place literally with plenty of room to grow. It's no wonder that there really are people who can't understand why anyone, given a choice, would not choose to give their children a chance to grow up in the country.

Not that there aren't problems. No place is perfect, and raising kids in the country is hardly worry-free. For one, there probably isn't a lifeguard down at the ol' swimmin' hole. Plenty of room to roam also means plenty of room to wander off and get into some sort of unsupervised trouble. The country's higher traffic fatality rate unfortunately includes kids who were walking or riding their bikes along the road when some vehicle barrelled out of control through the countryside.

No town, no place, no environment is absolutely perfect. People aren't perfect, either. Moving to the country isn't going to turn you into Superparent, transform Billy or Sis into an angel, or guarantee that your child won't get hurt, have a hard time, or grow up to be the worst prisoner in cell block 37. But at least in the country your kid isn't likely to become the victim of a drive-by shooting, get pressured into joining some street gang, or get mugged on the way to school or killed for his tennis shoes. If life is indeed a series of trade-offs, there are more than a few who believe that children allowed to grow up in the country get the best of the bargain.

School Days, School Ways

Any comparison of urban and rural schools has to begin with the difference in atmospheres. Local country schools don't need metal detectors, as so many city institutions do. Teachers in the country don't need experience in riot control to take charge of their classrooms.

And kids in the country aren't as likely to wander off to visit McDonald's or the nearest mall every time there's a test in math class.

This is not to say that country children are superior, or smarter, or inherently better-behaved. Rather, it's the surroundings and the comparatively homey small school atmosphere that makes much of the difference. There are fewer kids, so they're easier to control. Everyone knows each other, so there are fewer disciplinary problems. If a student in a small country school tries to cut class, everybody notices. There probably isn't a McDonald's next door to cut class and go to, or a convenient mall. In so many ways, getting an education in the country is far easier and far less complicated than surviving school in the city.

That's great, you say. You don't have to worry about Uzi's in the classroom. But what about the quality of education? It doesn't matter that the atmosphere in country schools is more conducive to learning if they don't provide the quality of education our kids need in today's world. And this is a legitimate concern.

During the last fifty years or so, exhaustive studies have looked at the differences between small schools and big schools. These studies aren't very helpful. Some of them have said in effect, "Yes, big schools are better." A significant number have also said, "No, little Pugsley is better off in a country school." How to decide?

A recent report of the Educational Resources Information Center (ERIC) of the U.S. Department of Education may shine a little light on the question. *What Is The Effect of Small-Scale Schooling on Student Achievement?* examined this contradictory research and offered some very revealing conclusions. The ERIC report found that those studies which favored large-school education tended to focus on "input variables," such as staff specialization and credentials, cost, teaching styles, and course offerings. But those studies which concentrated on "output variables," such as student achievement, found no meaningful differences between small school educations and large. According to the study: "[r]ecent studies of the effects of small-scale schooling on student achievement confirm that there is no systematic overall negative effect of small-scale organization on student achievement."

This is just a fancy way of saying that the quality of a child's education does not depend on how many other kids are enrolled in the school. While larger schools may, and often do, offer a more varied curriculum, there is no evidence to suggest that children with big-school educations do any better in life than those who attended small schools. Indeed, additional research suggests that "school climate" and "instructional leadership" makes sending children to small schools in a small town a more "productive strategy." To quote again from *The Effects of Small-Scale Schooling*:

> In contemporary life, young people too seldom form relationships within their communities that foster strong senses of identity. An education in a small rural school offers them clear opportunities to do so; it gives students a secure environment that increases their chances to be recognized as individuals.

In other studies, the Department of Education has found that "small schools, wherever they are, can help establish links between students and parents; it is more difficult for larger schools to achieve the same results." And, this brings us to perhaps the most important reason why kids might benefit from an education in the country. You. Their parents. Even though moving to the country won't turn you or your spouse into a parenting genius if you aren't one already, you'll have more time to be a parent there. The slower pace gives you time to spend with your children. Time to play games with them, read to them, answer their questions, listen to them. You'll be less stressed out, too, less likely to be irritable, less likely to be annoyed with your kids.

A lot of country parents reading this are probably responding, "Hey, buster, me and my kids live in the country, and I don't have time for squat, much less listening to Junior talk about his new pencil box." No doubt they're right. But as busy as they are now, would they have it any easier in, say, New York or one of its overcrowded suburbs?

Day Care

Two of the horrors of urban day care are finding facilities you can afford and finding people you feel comfortable leaving your youngsters with. In both cases the country offers some distinct advantages.

Like many other services, day care is commonly cheaper in the country. Rural costs vary from region to region, and even from town to town, but day care in the country is, in comparison to urban day care, reasonable and affordable. The options vary from small, state-sanctioned care centers to neighbors who regularly and informally baby-sit as a way of supplement their incomes. Almost without exception, you will find country day care to be less expensive than urban or suburban care.

As for the care-givers themselves, once again small town living works in your favor. Chances are that you or your neighbors already know the people who want to care for your children. You have a better chance to know what sort of people they are and what their history of caring for children is. You'll be better able to know if there's any reason to doubt or mistrust them. Nothing travels faster than rumor in a small town, and just the appearance of anything irregular will inevitably lead to suspicion and investigation.

"Grow Old With Me, The Best Is Yet To Be"

Generalizations about "old" country people as individuals are no more accurate than generalizations about anybody else. Nevertheless, there are a few things we do know about the lifestyle of the so-called "rural aged."

For one thing, large numbers of the country elderly own their own homes. Their houses are often plenty big for them, too, since in many cases their kids have grown up and moved out, leaving their empty rooms behind. Many of these homes are one-story—the rural aged don't like climbing stairs any more than the urban elderly do.

Older folks in the country don't have to give up much social life. Even those who don't drive a car can usually depend on informal support systems of family and friends to compensate for their lack of transportation. In fact, family contact with local relatives is as customary for older people in the country as it is for those in the city, and the frequency of contact with friends and neighbors is actually greater. Church membership and participation run high among older folks in the country, often constituting important aspects of social life.

Statistically, the rural elderly receive less than an average amount of medical care. In part, this is because medical care is not always nearby, but it may also have something to do with the independent streak exhibited by so many country people. They take pride in being on their own and taking care of things themselves, just as they always have done. And they may sneer at those who "run to the doctor for every little thing." This could be considered a good, mentally-healthy attitude, though it sometimes means forcing Grandpa and his broken leg to the nearest emergency room at gunpoint.

Many small-town elderly exhibit a positive, inspiring, down-to-earth outlook on life. Maybe it's because they're simply too wise or too experienced to be either starry-eyed optimists or gloomy melancholics. But they've also experienced the best that the country has to offer—the fresh air and clean water, the physical and emotional security, the neighborliness and community. It is more than possible that this healthy state of mind is also a reward for having lived a satisfying and fulfilling life in the country.

Trust Me

Perhaps the most fundamental denominator of country life is *trust*. People in small towns may not be inherently more trustworthy than those in the city, but the conditions and the context of life in the country dictate that people act more trustworthy and more trusting. There's nowhere to hide. You are much better able to know who your neighbors really are and better able to take their measure than if you lived in the anonymity of the city. In the country you almost have to live and act so that those around you can trust you. Since others have to live under the same conditions and circumstances, you are better able to know and trust them. Simply put, country people need to be more trustworthy and more trusting, because so much of rural life hinges on the cooperation and interdependence of friends, neighbors, kin, and acquaintances.

It really is a pretty simple way to live. And it works.

CHAPTER VIII

Very Real, Very Rural

❖

(A personal look at some of the immeasureable aspects of country living.)

In writing this book I've tried to stick largely to things that are quantifiable and verifiable about country living and to leave opinion and conjecture to others. I have especially wanted to avoid the reinforcement of stereotypes and uninformed assumptions in an effort to give those who are considering a move to the country a factual basis on which to proceed. Just the facts, ma'am, as Joe Friday might have said.

However, there are certain aspects of country living, of all living, that just can't be measured in facts and figures...aspects for which there are no hard-and-fast yardsticks of "good" or "bad"...instances where individual needs or preferences are not the only factors to consider when saying "yea" or "nay." No work on rural life would be complete without at least an attempt to take an intelligent look at some of these intangibles which contribute so significantly to the quality of life in the Boondocks.

True, I have no objective gauge with which to measure or compare these intangibles—to which I say, "so what"? A certain amount of opinion and conjecture may in fact be healthy. Am I biased in favor of life in the country? Naturally. Are there times when I suspect that we really have "paved Paradise and put up a parking lot" and that "we won't know what we've got till it's gone"? Yes, indeedy. There surely are and I surely do. But despite that, the subjects mentioned here will be presented with as much even-handedness as I can muster. Even though this final chapter is mostly concerned with those parts of life that can't be precisely measured, my goal, as much here as in the rest of this book, has been to draw as true a picture of the country as possible.

I suppose the most obvious, and one of the most immeasureable, aspects of country life is simply the country itself. The atmosphere, the environment, the surroundings. How do you gauge the smog index in a place that has no smog? How do you measure the feeling of waking up to the calm and quiet of a country morning, the freedom that comes from knowing that you're not subjected to all the rules and restrictions of city life? How can you communicate the pure pleasure that accompanies a solitary walk through the open countryside, the joy of digging up the first vegetable you've grown yourself? These are indescribable feelings, unique sensations for which there is no scale of comparison to rely on. Luckily, there's none needed. It's the same sort of feeling that turns a house into a home or makes your mom's cooking the best in the world. You can't measure a feeling like that. Even defining it is difficult. Yet there's nothing quite as real, and it contributes significantly to the quality of life of all those fortunate enough to experience it.

Writing a book about life in the country has let me appreciate all over again the many wonders of country life that, frankly, I'd grown to take for granted. The sight of cows grazing on a hillside, the sound of a woodpecker tap-tapping his beak into a nearby tree, the smell of freshly-plowed earth. All this somehow makes my life happier, more satisfying. I don't pretend to understand it, but I know it's true. And writing this book has been a welcome, personal reminder of just how much there is to be grateful for in the country.

Even as simple a thing as having pets makes me appreciate the freedom that comes with living in the country. It's not the same as owning animals in the city or suburbs, where you may have to keep Fluffy or Fido shut in the house all the time or tied to a tree. That's no way to keep pets and no way to enjoy them either. Can anyone doubt that most animals are much happier out in the country, where they can revel in the freedom, fresh air, and room to romp that simply can't be found in the asphalt jungle. I firmly believe that old Rover is a lot more content out where he can run free and chase rabbits and get burrs in his tail. Besides, happier pets make for happier owners. And you'll never have to use a pooper-scooper again.

Living in the country allows you to have pets of all sizes and breeds, from baby geese to full-grown horses. Hell, you can have an elephant, if you can afford the peanuts. Local zoning probably won't stop you from owning more exotic pets, either, though it might be a little embarrassing if your pet cheetah happens to make a meal out of the mailman. For the most part, nobody in a rural area is going to be too concerned with what kind or how many pets you have, so long as you're the one feeding them and they don't bite anybody too hard or dig up too many flower gardens.

Finally, living where you can own pets of all kinds under these conditions can even make you healthier. Scientists claim to have proof that owning pets can actually lower your heart rate, increase your chance of surviving an illness, lower your stress levels, and provide myriad other health advantages. It is true that pets may offer the same health benefits to their owners in the Big City. But, such benefits seem much more concrete in the country, where there is so much less stress to begin with.

As wonderful as it is to be able to wander scenic countrysides and as healthy as it may be to own happy pets, there are admittedly more important things to consider about life and about living it in the country. This brings us to what I think is the most vital of the quality-of-life intangibles of country living and one of the most important reasons to live and raise children in rural areas: the stability and security of small-town life and its contribution to the success and happiness of the people who live there.

One of the reasons rural places offer a more stable atmosphere is simply that there isn't a whole lot of physical change. In small towns, chances are that the buildings—the stores, the banks, the post offices, the restaurants are right where they've been for longer than you can remember. There's not apt to be much industrial development or new construction either, so the landscape will probably remain pretty much the same, too. If you grew up in the town, your kids may well go to school right where you did, maybe even sit at the same desks, play baseball or field hockey on the same field you played on, buy candy right where you bought it. A valid case can be made that a little progress wouldn't hurt some rural places, but there's also a lot of security in knowing that there are things in life you can count on. Stability in surroundings provides people with a firm base from which to proceed and grow.

That's part of the reason why even people themselves seem more stable in the country. It's also part of rural sociology. As I pointed out in the previous chapter, everybody knows everybody else in the country. No one can be anonymous in a small town, and everyone is made accountable for their behavior simply by virtue of being visible. Stable, civilized conduct is almost a necessary result.

And there's more. Families frequently remain living and working in the same area generation after generation. Even kids who grow up and move away for a time often find themselves back in the same general area. This family stability encourages community stability and helps bring a sense of security and continuity to the lives of all. Over the years, strong ties grow up between people: "My grandfather and yours used to be in business together." "His uncle almost married my mother when they were young." A whole way of life and thinking is forged and maintained. Much of this may be unspoken and even unthought-of, but it helps foster an everyday atmosphere that is remarkable in its stability and contributes much to people's sense of well-being and personal satisfaction.

I am convinced that growing up in the country prepares children well for life, no matter where they eventually choose to live it. The stability of country people, the security of the lifestyle, the opportunities for recognition and appreciation—all help build confidence and a positive outlook that translates into happiness and success in future years. Ask Johnny Carson, or Sam Walton, or any one of the millions of others, known and unknown, who have come from small towns and become successful members of the larger community.

You might also ask Larry Bird or Oprah Winfrey, who, despite less-than-ideal early home lives, persevered and thrived in highly competitive fields. While this certainly says a lot about their own personal strengths and abilities, I have no doubt that the small-town atmospheres into which they were born, including the close networks of friends and relatives, contributed much to everything they have accomplished.

The country teaches children that success is measured by more than victory, that it is participation as much as triumph, attempt and perseverance themselves as much as performance. Take the example of youth activities. Your son or daughter might not even make the team or pass the audition in the Big City, where so many kids compete for so few spots and where so little individual attention is available. But in a smaller, less-populated environment, they have much better chances of tasting the encouragement and appreciation that come from simply participating. No matter what their interests or hobbies may be, this early experience of success and recognition helps build confidence and a sense self-worth.

For children and adults alike, the relative isolation of small towns, even those with easy access to metropolitan areas, promotes a subtle we're-all-in-this-together feeling, a sense of true community and a trust in one's fellows that might seem terribly incongruous in an urban setting. Sociologists might disparagingly brand this as "provincialism" and call it an "island" or a "fortress" mentality, but that's not what small town life is like at all. More than anything else, people in small towns share a communal feeling that, whatever their individual differences, they are all members of the same team. They are full members of a Country Club of friends and neighbors who are willing and able to cooperate on a daily basis and eager to help each other out when called on.

I think it is obvious that people are happier and more successful, however you may define that word, when they live in a world of trust, stability, and mutual acceptance. And that such a life is more readily found in the country than in the city. It's not that I believe that country folk are "better" than their city counterparts. After all, like my Dad always said, people are people wherever and whenever. But, it's been my experience that the conditions of life in the country are much more likely to provide the peaceful and satisfied life so many of us are seeking.

In the introduction to this work, I stressed that I was by no means against the Big City or the people who live there, and I'll reemphasize that here. I can list many positive things about urban life. I've never been to a city or suburb where I haven't found someone or something to like. I've had some wonderful times in the City, and I have many good friends there who wouldn't—and shouldn't—dream of living anywhere else. I often miss the city and my friends a whole lot. All in all, the City is a great place to visit.

I just wouldn't want to live there.

The Country Club

APPENDIX A
Rural Counties, According to Beale

The Beale Codes discussed in Chapter 2 are used by the Economic Research Service to classify counties by their urban/rural character. The following counties are those which have received Beale Codes of six or greater, indicating that they are among the most rural counties in the country.

That's not to suggest that you should pack up and move to one of them without doing a little more research. The mosquito-and-alligator-infested swamp, the desert home of sidewinders and tarantulas, and the isolated stomping grounds of caribou and polar bears will all likely show up on this list. So, be advised.

Still, if you are looking for a truly rural place to settle, you will probably find it in one of the counties listed here.

❖

ALABAMA
Barbour
Bibb
Bullock
Butler
Cherokee
Chilton
Choctaw
Clarke
Clay
Cleburne
Coneguh
Coosa
Covington
Crenshaw
Cullman
De Kalb
Escambria
Fayette
Franklin
Geneva
Greene
Hale
Henry
Lamar
Lawrence
Limestone
Lowndes
Macon
Marengo
Marion
Monroe
Perry
Pickens
Pike
Randolph
Sumter
Tallapoosa
Washington
Wilcox
Winston

ALASKA
Aleutian Islands
Bethel
Bristol Bay Borough
Dillingham
Haines
Juneau
Kenai Peninsula
Ketchikan Gateway
Kobuk
Kodiak Island
Matanuska-Susitna
Nome
North Slope
Prince of Wales-
Outer Ketchikan
Sitka
Skagway-Yakutat-Angoon
Southeast Fairbanks
Valdez-Cordova
Wade Hampton
Wrangell-Petersburg
Yukon-Koyukuk

ARIZONA
Apache
Gila
Graham
Greenlee
La Paz
Santa Cruz

ARKANSAS
Arkansas
Ashley
Baxter
Boone
Bradley
Calhoun
Carroll
Chicot
Clark
Clay
Cleburne
Cleveland
Columbia
Conway
Cross
Dallas
Desha
Drew
Franklin
Fulton
Grant
Greene
Hempstead
Hot Spring
Howard
Independence
Izard
Jackson
Johnson
Lafayette
Lawrence
Lee
Lincoln
Little River
Logan
Madison
Marion
Monroe
Montgomery
Nevada
Newton
Ouachita
Perry
Pike
Poinsett
Polk
Pope
Prairie
Randolph
St. Francis
Scott
Searcy
Serier
Sharp
Stone
Van Buren
White
Woodruff
Yell

CALIFORNIA
Alpine
Amador
Calaveras
Colusa
Del Norte
Glenn
Inyo
Lake
Lassen
Mariposa
Modoc
Mono
Nevada
Plumas
San Benito
Sierra
Siskiyou
Tehama
Trinity
Tuolumne

COLORADO
Alamosa
Archuleta
Baca
Bent
Chaffee
Cheyenne
Clear Creek
Conejos
Costilla
Crowley
Custer
Delta
Dolores
Eagle
Elbert
Fremont
Garfield
Gilpin
Grand
Gunnison
Hinsdale
Huerfano
Jackson
Kiowa
Kit Carson
Lake
La Plata
Las Animas
Lincoln
Logan
Mineral
Moffat
Montezuma
Montrose
Morgan
Otero
Ouray
Park
Phillips
Pitkin
Prowers
Rio Blanco
Rio Grande
Routt
Saguache
San Juan
San Miguel
Sedgwick
Summit
Teller
Washington
Yuma

CONNECTICUT
none

DELAWARE
Sussex

FLORIDA
Baker
Calhoun
Citrus
Columbia
De Soto
Dixie0
Flagler
Franklin
Gilchrist
Glades
Gulf
Hamilton
Hardee
Hendry
Highlands
Holmes
Jackson
Jefferson
Lafayette
Levy
Liberty
Madison
Okeechobee
Putnam
Sumter
Suwannee
Taylor
Union
Wakulla
Walton
Washington

GEORGIA
Appling
Atkinson
Bacon
Baker
Banks
Bartow
Ben Hill
Berrien
Bleckley
Brantley
Brooks
Bryan
Bulloch
Burke
Calhoun
Camden
Candler
Carroll
Charlton
Chattooga
Clay
Clinch
Coffee
Colquitt
Cook
Crawford
Crisp
Dawson
Decatur
Dodge
Dooly
Early
Echols
Elbert
Dmanuel
Evans
Fannin
Franklin
Gilmer
Glascock
Gordon
Grady
Greene
Habersham
Hall
Hancock
Haralson
Harris
Hart
Heard
Irwon
Jasper
Jeff Davis
Jefferson
Jenkins
Johnson
Lamar

Appendix

Lanier	Wheeler	**ILLINOIS**	Randolph	Owen
Laurens	White	Alexander	Richland	Parke
Lincoln	Wilcox	Bond	Saline	Perry
Long	Wilkes	Brown	Schuyler	Pike
Lumpkin	Wilkinson	Bureau	Scott	Pulaski
McIntosh	Worth	Calhoun	Shelby	Putnam
Macon		Carroll	Stark	Randolph
Marion	**HAWAII**	Cass	Union	Ripley
Meriwether	Kauai	Christian	Wabash	Rush
Miller	Maui	Clark	Warren	Scott
Mitchell		Clay	Washington	Spencer
Monroe		Crawford	Wayne	Starke
Montgomery	**IDAHO**	Cumberland	White	Steuben
Morgan	Adams	De Witt		Sullivan
Murray	Bear Lake	Douglas	**INDIANA**	Switzerland
Olgethorpe	Benewah	Edgar	Adams	Union
Pickens	Bingham	Edwards	Benton	Vermillion
Pierce	Blaine	Effingham	Blackford	Wabash
Pike	Boise	Fayette	Brown	Warren
Polk	Bonner	Ford	Carroll	Washington
Pulaski	Boundary	Gallatin	Cass	Wells
Putnam	Butte	Greene	Clinton	White
Quitman	Camas	Hamilton	Crawford	
Rabun	Caribou	Hancock	Daviess	**IOWA**
Randolph	Cassia	Hardin	Decatur	Adair
Schley	Clark	Henderson	Dubois	Adams
Screven	Clearwater	Iroquois	Fayette	Allamakee
Seminole	Custer	Jasper	Fountain	Appanoose
Stephens	Elmore	Jefferson	Franklin	Audubon
Stewart	Franklin	Jo Daviess	Fulton	Benton
Sumter	Fremont	Johnson	Gibson	Boone
Talbot	Gem	Lawrence	Greene	Buchanan
Taliaferro	Gooding	Lee	Huntington	Buena Vista
Tattnall	Idaho	Livingston	Jackson	Butler
Taylor	Jefferson	Logan	Jasper	Calhoun
Telfair	Jerome	Macoupin	Jay	Carroll
Terrell	Latah	Marshall	Jefferson	Cass
Thomas	Lemhi	Mason	Jennings	Cedar
Tift	Lewis	Massac	Kosciusko	Cherokee
Toombs	Lincoln	Mercer	Lagrange	Chickasaw
Towns	Madison	Montgomery	Lawrence	Clarke
Treutlen	Minidoka	Moultrie	Marshall	Clay
Turner	Oneida	Ogle	Martin	Clayton
Twiggs	Owyhee	Perry	Miami	Crawford
Union	Payette	Piatt	Montgomery	Davis
Upson	Power	Pike	Newton	Decatur
Warren	Shoshone	Pope	Noble	Delaware
Washington	Teton	Pulaski	Ohio	Dickinson
Wayne	Valley	Putnam	Orange	Emmet
Webster	Washington			

The Country Club

Fayette
Floyd
Franklin
Fremont
Greene
Grundy
Guthrie
Hamilton
Hancock
Hardin
Harrison
Henry
Howard
Humboldt
Ida
Iowa
Jackson
Jasper
Jefferson
Jones
Keokuk
Kossuth
Louisa
Lucas
Lyon
Madison
Mahaska
Marion
Mills
Mitchell
Monona
Monroe
Montgomery
O'Broen
Osceola
Page
Palo Alto
Plymouth
Pocahontas
Poweshiek
Ringgold
Sac
Shelby
Sioux
Tama
Taylor
Union
Van Buren
Washington
Wayne

Winnebago
Winneshiek
Worth
Wright

KANSAS

Allen
Anderson
Atchison
Barber
Bourbon
Brown
Chase
Chautauqua
Cherokee
Cheyenne
Clark
Clay
Cloud
Coffee
Comanche
Decatur
Dickinson
Doniphan
Edwards
Elk
Ellis
Ellsworth
Finney
Ford
Franklin
Gove
Graham
Grant
Gray
Greeley
Greenwood
Hamilton
Harper
Harvey
Haskell
Hodgeman
Jackson
Jefferson
Jewell
Kearny
Kingman
Kiowa
Labette

Lane
Lincoln
Linn
Logan
Marion
Marshall
McPherson
Meade
Mitchell
Morris
Morton
Nemaha
Neosho
Ness
Norton
Osage
Osborne
Ottawa
Pawnee
Phillips
Pottawa-
  tomie
Pratt
Rawlins
Republic
Rice
Rooks
Rush
Russell
Scott
Seward
Sheridan
Sherman
Smith
Stafford
Stanton
Stevens
Sumner
Thomas
Trego
Wabaunsee
Wallace
Washington
Wichita
Wilson
Woodson

KENTUCKY

Adair

Allen
Anderson
Ballard
Barren
Bath
Bell
Boyle
Bracken
Breathitt
Breckinridge
Butler
Caldwell
Callaway
Carlisle
Carroll
Casey
Clay
Clinton
Crittenden
Cumberland
Edmonson
Elliott
Estill
Fleming
Floyd
Fulton
Gallatin
Garrard
Grant
Graves
Grayson
Green
Hancock
Harlan
Harrison
Hart
Henry
Hickman
Jackson
Johnson
Knott
Knox
Larue
Laurel
Lawrence
Lee
Letcher
Lewis
Lincoln
Livingston

Logan
Lyon
McCreary
McLean
Magoffin
Marion
Marshall
Martin
Mason
Meade
Menifee
Mercer
Metcalfe
Monroe
Montgomery
Morgan
Muhlenberg
Nelson
Nicholas
Ohio
Owen
Owsley
Pendleton
Perry
Pike
Powell
Pulaski
Robertson
Rockcastle
Rowan
Russell
Simpson
Spencer
Taylor
Todd
Trigg
Trimble
Union
Washington
Wayne
Webster
Whitley
Wolfe

LOUISIANA

Allen
Assumption
Avoyelles
Beauregard

Appendix 133

Bienville
Caldwell
Cameron
Catahoula
Claiborne
Colncordia
De Soto
East Carroll
East
  Feliciana
Evangeline
Franklin
Grant
Iberville
Jackson
Jefferson
  Davis
La Salle
Madison
Morehouse
Natchitoches
Plaquemines
Pointe
  Coupee
Red River
Richland
Sabine
St. Helena
St. James
Tensas
Union
Vermilion
West Carroll
West
  Feliciana
Winn

MAINE

Franklin
Hancock
Knox
Lincoln
Oxford
Piscataquis
Sagadahoc
Somerset
Waldo
Washington

MARYLAND

Caroline
Dorchester
Garrett
Kent
St. Marys
Somerset
Talbot
Wicomico
Worcester

**MASSA-
CHUSETTS**

Dukes
Nantucket

MICHIGAN

Alcona
Alger
Allegan
Alpena
Antrim
Arenac
Baraga
Barry
Benzie
Branch
Cass
Charlevoix
Cheboygan
Chippewa
Clare
Crawford
Delta
Dickinson
Emmet
Gladwin
Gogebic
Grand
  Traverse
Gratiot
Hillsdale
Houghton
Huron
Ionia
Iosco
Iron
Kalkaska

Keweenaw
  Lake
Leelanau
Luce
Mackinac
Manistee
Mason
Mecosta
Menominee
Missaukee
Montcalm
Mont-
  morency
Mewaygo
Oceana
Ogemaw
Ontonagon
Osceola
Oscoda
Otsego
Presque Isle
Roscommon
St. Joseph
Sanilac
Schoolcraft
Tuscola
Van Buren
Wexford

**MINNE-
SOTA**

Aitkin
Becker
Beltrami
Big Stone
Brown
Carlton
Cass
Chippewa
Clearwater
Cook
Cottonwood
Crow Wing
Dodge
Douglas
Faribault
Fillmore
Freeborn
Goodhue

Grant
Houston
Hubbard
Itasca
Jackson
Kanabec
Kandiyohi
Kittson
Koochiching
Lac Qui
  Parle
Lake
Lake of the
  Woods
Le Sueur
Lincoln
Lyon
McLeod
Mahnomen
Marshall
Martin
Meeker
Mille Lacs
Morrison
Murray
Nicollet
Nobles
Norman
Otter Tail
Pennington
Pine
Pipestone
Polk
Pope
Red Lake
Redwood
Renville
Rock
Roseau
Sibley
Steele
Stevens
Swift
Todd
Traverse
Wabasha
Wadena
Waseca
Watonwan
Wilkin

Yellow
  Medicine

MISSISSIPPI

Alcorn
Amite
Attala
Benton
Calhoun
Carroll
Chickasaw
Choctaw
Claiborne
Clarke
Clay
Copian
Covington
Franklin
George
Greene
Grenada
Holmes
Humphreys
Issaquena
Itawamba
Jasper
Jefferson
Jefferson
  Davis
Kemper
Lafayette
Lamar
Lawrence
Leake
Lincoln
Marion
Marshall
Monroe
Montgomery
Neshoba
Newton
Noxubee
Oktibbeha
Panola
Pearl River
Perry
Pike
Pontotoc
Prentiss

Quitman	Douglas	Schuyler	Pondera	Garden
Scott	Dunklin	Scotland	Powder River	Garfield
Sharkey	Gasconade	Shannon	Powell	Gosper
Simpson	Gentry	Shelby	Prairie	Grant
Smith	Grundy	Stoddard	Ravalli	Greeley
Smith	Harrison	Stone	Richland	Hamilton
Stone	Nenry	Sullivan	Roosevelt	Harlan
Sunflower	Hickory	Taney	Rosebud	Hayes
Tallahatchie	Holt	Texas	Sanders	Hitchcock
Tate	Howard	Vernon	Sheridan	Holt
Tippah	Howell	Warren	Stillwater	Hooker
Tishomingo	Iron	Washington	Sweet Grass	Howard
Tunica	Johnson	Wayne	Teton	Jefferson
Union	Knox	Webster	Toole	Johnson
Walthall	Laclede	Worth	Treasure	Kearney
Wayne	Lawrence	Wright	Valley	Keith
Webster	Lewis		Wheatland	Keya Paha
Wilkinson	Lincoln	**MONTANA**	Wibaux	Kimball
Winston	Linn	Beaverhead		Knox
Yalobusha	Livingston	Big Horn	**NEBRASKA**	Logan
Yazoo	McDonald	Blaine	Antelope	Loup
	Macon	Broadwater	Arthur	McPherson
MISSOURI	Madison	Carbon	Banner	Madison
Adail	Maries	Carter	Blaine	Merrick
Andrew	Mercer	Chouteau	Boone	Nance
Atchison	Miller	Custer	Box Butte	Hemaha
Audrain	Mississippi	Daniels	Boyd	Nuckolls
Barry	Moniteau	Dawson	Brown	Otoe
Barton	Montgomery	Deer Lodge	Burt	Pawnee
Bates	Morgan	Fallon	Butler	Perkins
Benton	New Madrid	Fergus	Cass	Phelps
Bollinger	Nodaway	Garfield	Cedar	Pierce
Butler	Oregon	Glacier	Chase	Platte
Caldwell	Osage	Golden Valley	Cherry	Polk
Callaway	Ozark	Granite	Cheyenne	Red Willow
Camden	Pemiscot	Hill	Clay	Richardson
Carroll	Perry	Jefferson	Colfax	Rock
Carter	Pettis	Judith Basin	Cuming	Saline
Cedar	Phelps	Lake	Custer	Saunders
Charlton	Pike	Liberty	Dawes	Seward
Clark	Polk	Lincoln	Dawson	Sheridan
Clinton	Putnam	McCone	Deuel	Sherman
Cooper	Ralls	Madison	Dixon	Sioux
Crawford	Randolph	Meagher	Dundy	Stanton
Dade	Reynolds	Mineral	Fillmore	Thayer
Dallas	Ripley	Musselshell	Franklin	Thomas
Daviess	St. Clair	Park	Frontier	Thruston
De Kalp	St. Francois	Petroleum	Furnas	Valley
Dent	Ste. Genevieve	Phillips	Gage	Wayne
	Saline			Webster

Wheeler
York

NEVADA

Churchill
Douglas
Elko
Esmeralda
Eureka
Humboldt
Lander
Lincoln
Lyon
Mineral
Nye
Pershing
Storey
White Pine

NEW HAMPSHIRE

Belknap
Carroll
Coos
Sullivan

NEW JERSEY

none

NEW MEXICO

Catron
Colfax
De Baca
Grant
Guadalupe
Harding
Hidalgo
Lincoln
Los Alamos
Luna
Mora
Quay
Rio Arriba
Roosevelt

Sandoval
San Miguel
Sierra
Socorro
Taos
Torrance
Union

NEW YORK

Allegheny
Chenango
Columbia
Delaware
Essex
Franklin
Hamilton
Lewis
Otsego
Schoharie
Schuyler
Seneca
Sullivan
Wyoming
Yates

NORTH CAROLINA

Alleghany
Anson
Ashe
Avery
Beaufort
Bertie
Bladen
Brunswick
Caldwell
Camden
Carteret
Caswell
Chatham
Cherokee
Chowan
Clay
Columbus
Currituck
Dare
Duplin
Gates
Graham

Granville
Greene
Harnett
Haywood
Henderson
Hertford
Hoke
Hyde
Jackson
Johnston
Jones
Lee
McDowell
Macon
Madison
Martin
Mitchell
Montgomery
Moore
Nash
Northampton
Pamlico
Pasquotank
Pender
Perquimans
Person
Polk
Richmond
Rutherford
Sampson
Scotland
Stanly
Surry
Swain
Transylvania
Tyrrell
Vance
Warren
Washington
Watauga
Wilkes
Yancey

NORTH DAKOTA

Adams
Barnes
Benson
Billings

Bottineau
Bowman
Burke
Cavalier
Dickey
Divide
Dunn
Eddy
Emmons
Foster
Golden Valley
Grant
Griggs
Hettinger
Kidder
La Moure
Logan
McHenry
McIntosh
McKenzie
McLean
Mercer
Mountrail
Nelson
Oliver
Pembina
Pierce
Ramsey
Ransom
Renville
Richland
Rolette
Sargent
Sheridan
Sioux
Slope
Stark
Steele
Strutsman
Towner
Traill
Walsh
Wells
Williams

OHIO

Adams
Brown
Champaign

Clinton
Coshocton
Darke
Fayette
Gallia
Guernsey
Hardin
Harrison
Henry
Highland
Hocking
Holmes
Jackson
Knox
Logan
Meigs
Mercer
Monroe
Morgan
Morrow
Noble
Ottawa
Paulding
Perry
Pike
Preble
Putnam
Shelby
Van Wewrt
Vinton
Williams
Wyandot

OKLAHOMA

Adair
Alfalfa
Atoka
Beaver
Beckham
Blaine
Bryan
Caddo
Cherokee
Choctaw
Cimarron
Coal
Cotton
Craig
Custer

Delaware
Dewey
Ellis
Gravin
Grady
Grant
Greer
Harmon
Harper
Haskell
Hughes
Jefferson
Johnston
Kingfisher
Kiowa
Latimer
Le Flore
Lincoln
Love
McCurtain
McIntosh
Major
Marshall
Mayes
Murray
Noble
Nowata
Okfuskee
Ottawa
Pawnee
Pittsburg
Pontotoc
Pushmataha
Roger Mills
Seminole
Texas
Tillman
Washita
Woods
Woodward

OREGON
Baker
Clatosp
Columbia
Crook
Curry
Gilliam
Grant

Harney
Hood River
Jefferson
Lake
Lincoln
Malheur
Morrow
Sherman
Tillamook
Union
Wallowa
Wasco
Wheeler

PENNSYL-VANIA
Armstrong
Bedford
Bradford
Cameron
Clarion
Clearfield
Clinton
Elk
Forest
Fulton
Greene
Huntingdon
Jefferson
Juniata
McKean
Mifflin
Montour
Pike
Potter
Snyder
Sullivan
Susquehanna
Tioga
Union
Warren
Wayne

RHODE ISLAND
none

SOUTH CAROLINA
Abbeville
Allendale
Bamberg
Barnwell
Beaufort
Calhoun
Cherokee
Chester
Chesterfield
Clarnedon
Colleton
Darlington
Dillon
Edgefield
Fairfield
Georgetown
Greenwood
Hampton
Horry
Jasper
Kershaw
Lancaster
Lee
McCormick
Marion
Marlboro
Newberry
Oconee
Saluda
Union
Williamsburg

SOUTH DAKOTA
Aurora
Beadle
Bennett
Bon Homme
Brookings
Brule
Buffalo
Butte
Campbell
Charles Mix
Clark
Clay
Codington

Corson
Custer
Davison
Day
Dueul
Douglas
Edmunds
Fall River
Faulk
Grant
Gregory
Haakon
Hamlin
Hand
Hanson
Harding
Hughes
Hutchinson
Hyde
Jackson
Jerauld
Jones
Kingsbury
Lake
Lawrence
Lincoln
Lyman
McCook
McPherson
Marshall
Meade
Mellette
Miner
Moody
Perkins
Potter
Roberts
Sanborn
Shannon
Spink
Stanley
Sully
Todd
Tripp
Turner
Union
Walworth
Yankton
Ziebach

TENNESSEE
Bedford
Benton
Bledsoe
Campbell
Cannon
Carroll
Chdster
Claiborne
Clay
Cocke
Crockett
Cumberland
Dacatur
DeKalb
Dyer
Fayette
Fentress
Franklin
Giles
Greene
Grundy
Hamblen
Hancock
Haredman
Hardin
Haywood
Henderson
HEnry
Hickman
Houston
Humphreys
Jackson
Johnson
Lake
Lauderdale
Lawrence
Lewis
Lincoln
Loudon
McMinn
McNairy
Macon
Marshall
Meigs
Moore
Obion
Overton
Perry

Appendix 137

Pickett	Collings-	Hopkins	Oldham	Wilson
Polk	worth	Houston	Palo Pinto	Winkler
Rhea	Colorado	Hudspeth	Panola	Wise
Scott	Comanche	Hutchinson	Parmer	Wood
Smith	Concho	Irion	Pecos	Yoakum
Stewart	Cooke	Jack	Polk	Young
Trousdale	Cottle	Jackson	Presidio	Zapata
Van Buren	Crane	Jasper	Rains	Zavala
Warren	Crockett	Jeff Davis	Reagan	
Wayne	Crosby	Jim Hogg	Real	**UTAH**
Weakley	Culberson	Jopnes	Red River	Beaver
White	Dallam	Karnes	Reeves	Box Elder
	Dawson	Kendall	Refugio	Carbon
TEXAS	Deaf Smith	Kenedy	Roberts	Daggett
Anderson	Delta	Kent	Robertson	Duchesne
Andrews	Dewitt	Kerr	Runnels	Emery
Aransas	Dickens	Kimble	Rusk	Grafield
Archer	Dimmit	King	Sabine	Grand
Armstrong	Donley	Kinney	San Augus-	Iron
Atascosa	Duval	Knox	tine	Juab
Austin	Eastland	Lamb	San Jacinto	Kane
Bailey	Edwards	Lampasas	San Saba	Millard
Bandera	Erath	La Salle	Schleicher	Morgan
Bastrop	Falls	Lavaca	Scurry	Piute
Baylor	Fannin	Lee	Shackelford	Rich
Bee	Fayette	Leon	Shelby	San Juan
Blanco	Fisher	Limestone	Sherman	Sanpete
Borden	Floyd	Lipscomb	Somervell	Sevier
Bosque	Foard	Live Oak	Starr	Summit
Brewster	Franklin	Llano	Stephens	Tooele
Briscoe	Freestone	Loving	Sterling	Uintah
Brooks	Frio	Lynn	Stonewall	Wasatch
Brown	Gaines	McCulloch	Sutton	Washington
Burleson	Garza	McMullen	Swisher	Wayne
Burnet	Gillespie	Madison	Terrell	
Caldwell	Glasscock	Marion	Terry	
Calhoun	Goliad	Martin	Throckmorton	**VERMONT**
Callahan	Gonzales	Mason	Titus	Addison
Camp	Grimes	Medina	Trinity	Bennington
Carson	Hall	Menard	Tyler	Caledonia
Cass	Hamilton	Milam	Upshur	Essex
Castro	Hansford	Mills	Uptopn	Franklin
Chambers	Hardeman	Mitchell	Uvalde	LaMoille
Cherokee	Hartley	Montague	Van Zandt	Orange
Childress	Haskell	Moore	Ward	Orleans
Clay	Hemphill	Morris	Washington	Rutland
Cochran	Henderson	Motley	Wharton	Washington
Coke	Hill	Newton	Wheeler	Windham
Coleman	Hockley	Nolan	Wilbarger	Windsor
	Hood	Ochiltree	Willacy	

VIRGINIA
Accomack
Alleghany
Amelia
Appomattox
Bath
Bedford
Bland
Brunswick
Buchanan
Buckingham
Caroline
Carrroll
Charlotte
Clarke
Craig
Culpeper
Cumberland
Dickenson
Essex
Fauquier
Floyd
Franklin
Giles
Grayson
Greensville
Halifax
Highland
Isle of Wight
King and Queen
King George
King William
Lancaster
Lee
Louisa
Lunenburg
Madison
Mathews
Mecklenburg
Middlesex
Nelson
Northampton
Northumberland
Nottoway
Orange
Page
Patrick
Prince Edward
Pulaski
Rappahannock
Richmond
Rockbridge
Russell
Shenandoah
Smyth
Soughampton
Spotsylvania
Surry
Sussex
Tazewell
Warren
Westmoreland
Wise
Wythe

WASHINGTON
Adams
Asotin
Columbia
Douglas
Ferry
Grafield
Island
Jefferson
Kittitas
Klickitat
Lincoln
Mason
Okanogan
Pacific
Pend Oreille
San Juan
Skamania
Stevens
Wahkiakum

WEST VIRGINIA
Barbour
Berkeley
Boone
Braxton
Calhoun
Clay
Doddridge
Fayette
Gilmer
Grant
Greenbrier
Hampshire
Hardy
Jackson
Jefferson
Lewis
Lincoln
Logan
McDowell
Mason
Mingo
Monroe
Morgan
Nicholas
Pendleton
Pleasants
Pocahontas
Preston
Randolph
Ritchie
Roane
Summers
Taylor
Tucker
Tyler
Upshur
Webster
Wetzel
Wirt
Wyoming

WISCONSIN
Adams
Ashland
Barron
Bayfield
Burfalo
Burnett
Clark
Columbia
Crawford
Door
Dunn
Florence
Forest
Grant
Green
Green Lake
Iowa
Iron
Jackson
Juneau
Kewaunee
Lafayette
Langlade
Lincoln
Marinette
Marquette
Monroe
Oconto
Oneida
Pepin
Pierce
Polk
Price
Richland
Rusk
Sauk
Sawyer
Shawano (inc. Menominee)
Taylor
Trempealeau
Vernon
Vilas
Washburn
Waupaca
Waushara

WYOMING
Big Horn
Campbell
Carbon
Converse
Crook
Fremont
Goshen
Hot Springs
Johnson
LIncoln
Niobrara
Park
Platte
Sheridan
Sublette
Teton
Uinta
Washakie
Weston